# SUBTRACTION

## The Subtle Art of Unleashing Boundless Innovation

Sujith Ravindran, Fabio Salvadori, Elliot Leavy

*To the daring soul who walks the inner road to the extraordinary*

# Table of Contents


Preface — 3

Introduction — 13

Part I - Innovation Matters — 16

   1.1 A World Shaped by Innovation — 21

   1.2 The Struggles of Innovation — 29

   1.3 What is Innovation? — 39

Part II - Awareness Informs Configuration — 44

   2.1 The Being Innovator — 49

   2.2 Configuration — 53

   2.3 Awareness Informs Configuration — 61

   2.4 Anandamaya Kosha - The Violet Layer — 75

   2.5 Vigyanamaya Kosha - The Blue Layer — 85

   2.6 Manomaya Kosha - The Yellow Layer — 95

   2.7 Pranamaya Kosha - The Orange Layer — 105

   2.8 Annamaya Kosha - The Red Layer — 1117

   2.9 The Wholistic Nature of the Being Innovator — 127

Part III - Awareness Fuels Innovation — 134

   3.1 Becoming the Being Innovator — 147

   3.2 How Awareness Fuels the Innovator's Journey — 159

   3.3 The Pitfalls of Bypassing the Innovator's Journey — 179

   3.4 Summing up the Innovator's Journey — 215

Closing the Circle — 217

Epilogue — 219

# Acknowledgments

Thank you to my two kids, Adya and Reya, who embody the spirit of boundless innovation. Since I am not their employer, I often wish they would take a break sometimes from their relentless innovations. To the 5th member of my family, Kala, the young cat who kept me company every night while I enjoyed my writing. She prefers YouTube to this manuscript but never complained. Thanks also to Fabio and Elliot for their unconditional willingness to join me in my world of mystical magic.

*Sujith Ravindran*

Thanks to Lorena, who always held with love the space for me to follow my dream, to the point of moving a thousand miles away to let me work evenings and weekends. Thanks to my family and closest friends, who kindly stopped asking me when the book was coming out two years ago. And thanks to my writing partners for their relentless commitment to understanding my inflexion when no speech-to-text transcription software could.

*Fabio Salvadori*

Thanks to my mother, Lorraine, who always made sure I kept my world from being small.

*Elliot Leavy*

# Preface

Fabio Salvadori

*"Are we leaving ourselves behind?"*

It was the Spring of 2017 when this question manifested in my mind. At that time, I didn't know it was the seed that would lead years later to this book.

As a creative technologist - my role back then - I was obviously in awe of the exhilarating speed of innovation in every field of our life. People and companies around the world were, and still are, pushing the boundaries of what is possible. Yet, at the same time, something was troubling me, but I couldn't understand what it was.

Around that time, a friend suggested I read *Guns, Germs, and Steel: The Fates of Human Societies* by Jared Diamond. It's a huge but compelling tome on the history of humankind. I was particularly struck by a passage in the book where Diamond describes technological innovation as an autocatalytic process, meaning "one that speeds up at a rate that increases with time because the process catalyzes itself". When I read that, I clearly remember thinking that if we kept accelerating at some point, we would probably leave ourselves behind. And maybe it was already happening, at least for some. While a few visionary people were preparing to travel to Mars, many human beings had no shoes to walk. From that moment on, that question remained stuck in my head: are we leaving ourselves behind?

In me, there was a growing feeling that this accelerating race towards the future was leaving behind larger parts of humanity. And even worse, also part of our humanness. Plus, while the impact that innovations have had on our lives' quality is undeniable, the challenges for humanity that those same innovations create were, and still are, getting bigger and bigger. From climate change to wealth disparity, just to name two.

*Is this an intrinsic characteristic of innovation, or is it possible to change the way we innovate, so we won't leave anyone behind?*

To find an answer to this question, I took a step back from my job as a creative technologist and began a journey that would change me profoundly, inside and outside.

Innovation has been part of my life since my school years, even if the word was not part of my dictionary at that time. I was not fascinated by new technologies per se. To be honest, I just loved to solve problems. And computer science gave me the opportunities and the tools to do that. I thought I could solve any issue with some good ideas, a few code lines, and a powerful computer. This focus on impact more than on the technology has been the underlying driver of my nonlinear professional career. I was drawn by challenges in which I could use my logic, knowledge and skills to create a solution. And I was good at it.

However, my logic and knowledge were useless in answering the more profound questions lingering in my mind.

I needed to find new ways.

The first breakthrough in my quest happened a few months later during a three-day summit on innovation organized by Being At Full Potential at the Institute of Noetic Sciences in Petaluma, California. For two days, I did my best to do the work and contribute to the conversations. I dug deep in my knowledge and experiences, yet I felt I was running in circles and going nowhere. On the third day, tired and frustrated, I stopped trying. I surrendered to the fact that my effort wasn't working and just enjoyed the place and the company. And then, the magic happened. As soon as I let go of the belief that I needed to know more to see better, ideas began to flow. It was my first experience of the power of subtraction.

The adventure of this book started in those days, after a conversation with Sujith. It was also the beginning of my inner journey of which this book is, in many ways, the recount. In the four years since then, I had to unlearn as much as I have learned. I questioned my beliefs and assumptions about everything. The search for new ways of innovating became a quest for my identity. Every step on the outside required an equivalent transformation on the inside.

This was my second breakthrough; to innovate the world, I needed to innovate myself first.

The very human nature of this endeavour made the writing of this book a very long and winding journey, one full of inspiring conversations, extensive research, changes, resets and pivots, bursts of creativity and long weeks of nothing. Every time I thought we had figured things out, I found myself lost again, unable to grasp something that I felt was there but still hidden from my eyes. Though the more I practiced letting go and trusting the wisdom of the Universe, the more I could open up to the unexpected and allow for this book to find its way into the world. Insights and ideas manifested in the most unexpected ways. A napkin in a pizza place, a conversation during a pilgrimage on the Italian hills, a meditation at dawn on a beach in Goa, an afternoon playing with my niece, or a coaching session with a client. A constellation of signs and omens that guided me towards a simple yet powerful truth.

We all are born innovators.

We all have unlimited creative potential that allows us to see everything as an opportunity to create something new and impactful.

This book is an invitation to embrace your innate potential to innovate and join us in the inner journey to awaken the magnificent innovator within you.

Sujith Ravindran

*"This was the most difficult book I have ever written."*

Not because it was written together with two futurists and innovation giants. My co-authors are the most amazing brains when it comes to offering something meaningful to humanity and the planet. They are the most awakened hearts when it comes to wanting to self-realize their own potential. Co-creating with them has been an easy and rewarding experience.

The challenge with this book has been in translating the core theme of awareness into the current context of innovation. That was acrobatic. While writing I constantly wondered, how do I maintain the science of awareness with integrity while making it relevant to the world of innovation? How do I not compromise on the essence and language of the timeless wisdom while reaching the reader where she is, rather than expect her to meet us where we are?

The answer was found by entering into an active dialogue with innovators and leaders. Over the years, I have taken several of them through an awareness journey and listened carefully to their experiments with awareness in the innovation space. Only when I could convey my truth to the target reader in a way she understood did we enter it into this manuscript.

## *The Era of Innovating Innovation*

The traditional audience of this book is used to a certain innovation process. If you are a regular soul, often you reflect on your daily innovations. If you are a craftsman, you are bound to respond to customers and apply trial and error. If you are an innovation driven organization, chances are you embark on extensive consumer research and product development processes. If you are an activist, you are constantly looking for ways to disrupt or leapfrog the status quo.

The time for *innovating* innovation has come. What else would explain this huge surge of interest in spiritual and metaphysical matters among innovators? Whether in the field of technology, social, commercial or governance, there is an active exploration going on about accessing previously unseen layers of human thought. Every month I am called to address at least one platform on the mind and the self. On all these platforms, I notice enthusiasm for reframing our understanding of the self in order to boost our innovation ability.

Many innovators seem willing to innovate their innovation processes. The typical approach of activists is to take a route that is against the status quo. That means engaging all stakeholders who are against the establishment and evolving a route that is amenable to most partners.

The traditional innovation process within organizations, rightly so, begins with a needs analysis. In this step, they study the real and perceived needs of their stakeholders and generate an appropriate problem definition. This is usually followed by concept development, prototyping, alpha and beta productization and eventual industrialization. This process is usually true for a product or a service innovation. Practices like Design Thinking and AGILE have added an inspiring amount of advantage to the traditional innovation process within organizations.

I have noticed these processes taught in the most elite business schools and practiced in the most innovative companies on the planet. I have also realized that the ROI of the current innovation approaches has peaked. This is asking us to *innovate* innovation itself.

The new innovation process will take a different route. It will focus less on 'doing' innovation and more on 'being' innovator. The new process will start and end where the traditional process did, that is with needs analysis and industrialization respectively. But the arc of the new process will take us elsewhere in our search for innovation; our 'being' will take the route of intentioning, illumination, imagination, infusion and materialization before arriving at industrialization.

This process will focus more on the innovator than on the process. When we harness the infinite human potential that remains unrealized within each individual, we can turn them into radical innovators.

This is not a far-fetched idea. Haven't you ever wondered why kids are so innovative while adults aren't? I have.

In fact, I know that I used to be innovative. Very innovative. That was a long time ago. When I was a child.

I could find a solution to any problem. An answer to any question. Sometimes multiple solutions or answers to every problem or question that arose. In fact, often I didn't even see things as a problem, just as another setup to play. Even innovate my way out of a problem before the problem existed. I knew that I was not the only one. Most children around me did the same. It was our normal.

Then something changed. I grew up. And with that I lost the magic. My innovations – if any – became very linear and mundane. Predictable. Incremental. Often even selfish.

Growing up I learned the science behind this personal degradation. I learned that my capacity to innovate depended upon my awareness.

When I was in a worldly, wakeful awareness, I could barely innovate. When I was in a whole-spectrum awareness, I could innovate radically.

Why is that?

Radical innovation is a product of the collaboration between man and the Universe. Should you seek an incremental innovation, you can rely on your individual resources. On the strength of your intellect you can improve upon what exists already. With a little imagination, you can turn a workbench into a toy table. Or an internal hard disk into an external one.

However, to create something out of nothing takes a higher mind, a mind formed by the union of the individual mind and the Universal mind. How else do you explain the 'sourcing' of Einstein? Or the 'channelling' of Carlos Santana? Or the 'Eureka' of Archimedes? Those breakthroughs do not come from the limited individual mind. According to those innovators, there is a higher place from which their innovations originate.

However, the mythology of such radical innovations says that such innovations are accidental. They are considered to 'happen' to certain individuals at unexpected moments.

However the sages believe differently. They recognize that each individual has the ability to connect with and harness the Universal mind. Thus, each one of us has the potentiality to limitlessly create the most radical innovations. This book is an attempt to demystify this secret.

# SUBTRACTION

# Elliot Leavy

*"2020 was a year where the world ground to a halt."*

Here in the UK, I was one of the first to be furloughed for what would become a surreal nine months. Nine months in which I lounged around, read a lot and wrote here and there about what was happening in the world of tech. It was nine months of pausing, thinking, and reassessing our world. My understanding of how our economies, democracies, and how our general social and business interactions functioned was suddenly up for negotiation. Knowledge that at one time seemed grounded in reality suddenly failed to reflect it whatsoever.

A world turned upside down, all because of some invisible threat from a land far far away. In this I was reminded of the plot of legendary sci-fi writer John Wyndham's *The Kraken Wakes,* which begins with fireballs falling from the sky and landing in the ocean. These mysterious orbs are in fact the start of a subterranean invasion by beings from another planet - beings which the protagonist, nor the reader are once given an inkling of their appearance. Despite their elusive presence, the aliens' arrival alters the future of mankind, rendering it totally unrecognisable to those who knew what was before.

As I am sure many others have noticed since the beginning of the pandemic, questions such as 'How would we recover?, Would we ever return to normal?, Do we want to return to normal?' leapt to the forefront of everyone's mind. With GDPs resetting to values not seen in decades, and graphs showing drops in wealth that seemed as comical as incomprehensible, it seemed that these questions were all foregone conclusions.

We would not be able to recover, we would not return to normal - at least 2019 normal - whether we liked it or not. Questions still lingered in the air, "What did this mean for what came next? Would it be better? Would it be worse? Would it remain the same but with an additional dose of hand-wringing over hand washing?" No one knew.

I still do not know the answer to these questions. I see new opportunities arising for experimentation in spaces such as Universal Basic Income (of which I was never a fan, and after nine months of furlough remain so), new problems in regards to data privacy as previous concerns around what was happening in the digital space became superseded by a real-life threat in the physical one. On top of that, a whole world of new cybersecurity threats continued to reveal themselves as we moved toward a cashless society filled with shoddy apps created in haste to deal with the current situation.

But amongst all of this worry, it took but a brief encounter courtesy of Elon Musk - who on the day I write this leapfrogged Amazon's Jeff Bezos to become the richest man in the world - that provided some much needed reprieve.

Late one night in the garden, thinking I had had one too many negronis on yet another furloughed day, I looked up to see what appeared to be the stars aligned. Not in the astrological sense, but in sense that these stars were following each other, in total I counted approximately fifty moving in a straight line across the black sky.

The next day I discovered this was not some cocktail-induced-hallucination, but Starlink, the satellite internet constellation being constructed by Musk's SpaceX that aims to provide low-cost, high speed broadband connectivity globally.

Even amongst all the tedious melancholy that would give *Groundhog Day* a run for its money, there they were, newly launched satellites lighting up the sky for all to see. Even though I had felt that everything had stopped and no progress was to be made it turned out that the opposite was in fact true, emblazoned, up there in the stars (to the annoyance of astronomers everywhere). And, unlike in the *Kraken Wakes,* these lights in the sky were not the harbingers of imminent invasion, but of ongoing innovation.

I have written about and for many innovators across the globe. Professors, policy makers, heads of major companies and smaller startups. There is something which connects all of them somehow, no matter where they are from. It is something that cannot be put down to simple ambition or the workings of lady luck. It is a certain outlook, of dreaming bigger than big, having not only a finger on the pulse of the current zeitgeist, but also feeling for the one that comes next.

Putting such a mindset into practice is where this book comes into play. For, at a time when we need innovation the most, we find it lacking. We are in many ways stuck up a proverbial creek without a paddle, worse still, we do not even know what a creek is, let alone where our lost selves are situated on it.

The philosophies which are central to this text are honest attempts to understand what makes the innovator's mindset so exceptional. Or perhaps better still, to prove how unexceptional they are, and how, given time and the right mindset, it is possible for anyone to become an exceptional innovator.

# Introduction

"Necessity is the mother of invention," Plato seems to have said.

If that is true, this should be an exceptionally inventive period considering we are in a moment of necessity like never before in post-war human history.

At a purely human level, many are struggling to make ends meet. Others are neglecting self-care and self-realization. Relationships are a struggle to maintain and nurture. We are increasingly disconnected from our communities and societies. Economic inequity is on the rise. Political apathy and ideological polarization have been growing worldwide. Ecological devastation has been unprecedented.

To compound matters, past innovations have been spawning a wake of new necessities. More and more, evidence shows us that the way we are innovating today cannot provide answers to the increasing complexity of the challenges ahead of us. If there is one thing that the COVID pandemic of 2020 has proven, it is that we need to disrupt not just innovation but also our entire way of living. In a word, everything.

Some institutions have been responding to these challenges with noble intentions. Many initiatives have been taken to rethink our current societal and global systems.

For years now, most countries and leading institutions have been championing the UN Sustainable Development Goals to create a more equitable and sustainable world. We have the Paris Agreement to tackle climate change. More recently, we have noticed the "Great Reset" of capitalism proposed by the World Economic Forum to revamp all aspects of our societies and economies. Or the recent conversations around a Marshall Plan 2.0 to help the world recover from this pandemic. Indian industry is mandated to extend 2% of their profits to Corporate Social Responsibility as a means towards social development.

All these intentions seem noble, virtuous, and incredibly well-articulated. Yet, the reality is that most of these initiatives are yet to yield as promised. The ongoing initiatives have failed to deliver the urgent transformation that they were designed for.

The time for incremental and self-serving innovations is up. If we are to alter the arc of human evolution, we are called for a completely different, inside-out approach to innovation.

Unless we focus on the essence of the human being - at an individual and collective level - by doing the essential work of subtracting all the mental limitations we have acquired through life, our innovations will not create the transformation the world seeks.

We must begin by expanding our awareness. This has two benefits; firstly, expanding awareness births radical innovations, and secondly, it always leads to altruistic innovations.

And these are precisely the two qualities of innovation we need to save the world; radical and altruistic.

"As long as you are attempting to be creative within the field of your conditioning, you cannot be creative," J Krishnamurti famously said.

The more we peel away the layers of our conditioning acquired through a lifetime of experiences, the more we are able to expand our awareness. Consequently, the more we can access the field of pure potentiality from which radical innovations can emerge.

"Creativity and Ego cannot go together. If you free yourself from the comparing and jealous mind, your creativity opens up endlessly. Just as water springs from a fountain, creativity springs from every moment. You must not be your own obstacle." These words of Jeong Kwang, Buddhist

Monk and Chef, accurately speaks to how by transcending our ego, we can become a fountain of altruistic innovations that can transform humanity and the planet.

As we expand our awareness, we come in touch with faculties that have remained unexpressed before. These faculties are crucial to boundless innovations. However, it is not sufficient to simply access these faculties. That is only half the story.

For innovations to create impact, we must first materialize the inventions by fully integrating these faculties into our innovation process. In doing so, we will fully unleash the power of boundless innovations. We will create radical and altruistic innovations that will make a positive impact on everyone and everything.

The good news is that we all can do it. We are all born innovators. We all have unlimited creative potential that allows us to see everything as an opportunity to change what exists and create something new and impactful.

This book is an invitation to embrace an inward journey that will take you beyond the limitations of the human mind to awaken your boundless innovation potential.

# Part I:

Innovation Matters

On 28 November 1979, a sightseeing aircraft carrying 257 people crashed into the side of a volcano on Ross Island in Antarctica. The tragedy, remembered as the Mount Erebus disaster, was caused by a mismatch between what the pilots thought the flight path was and what it actually was supposed to be. Briefed with the wrong map and guided along a different path by the computer, disaster struck before the team had any way of turning around.

The pilot, Captain Jim Collins, and co-pilot Greg Cassin were both experienced in their field, yet this was the first time either of them had ventured to the world's most southern continent. 19 days prior to the disaster, they had both attended a briefing in which they were given a copy of the previous flight's flight plan.

The flight plan, followed by the majority of the previous 13 flights, was, however, incorrect. Although calculated correctly, it had been inputted into the computer incorrectly, meaning that those previous flights, which thought they were flying the correct route, were, in fact, flying an incorrect route the entire time.

What acted as the catalyst for disaster for this flight, in particular, was an external force outside of anyone's control. Outside of the plane, a layer of cloud had blended in with the white snow atop of the volcano. This lack of contrast, known as whiteout, meant that there was no warning of the flight's impending fate, and the plane collided into the side of the volcano at approximately 12:49 pm, killing all 257 passengers and crew on board.

The chilling tale was made even more eerie by the lack of awareness of those onboard of what was approaching. Today, one can still find photographs taken by passengers minutes before the crash, oblivious to their doom and still enjoying their flight above the same land which would be their demise.

***

In today's uncertain world, our shared problems have deep roots from which they continue to grow, and we continue to apply the same methodologies and processes that solved problems of the past onto the problems of the present – with lacklustre results.

To say that this approach is ill-advised would be an understatement. At its best, trusting in systems and methodologies that are no longer relevant to the problems at hand can prove tedious. At worst, it can be deadly, as we learned from the Mount Erebus disaster. The crash, still the source of a bitter blame game today, was the result of a miscommunication between the pilots' perception and reality, induced by a change they were unaware had occurred.

This is often true when it comes to our innovation practices. We tend to stick to approaches even when they no longer apply. We may think that they still apply, but that does not change the fact that they do not. Navigating with the wrong map, even if in previously understood territories, can lead to disaster.

It is clear, then, that a different approach is needed. Why?

Because innovation, in short, matters. It should be difficult to disagree with this statement. Innovation is the sustaining force behind human existence, enriching our time here on earth and setting the stage for those who come next. Hence, innovation not only matters but is essential to the human condition and existence, intrinsically tied to the development of our beliefs, motivations and actions. Innovation, then, is our path into the future, the human equivalent of biological evolution.

But innovation is much faster than evolution: it keeps accelerating at an increasing pace. Which, paradoxically, is why innovation is also one of the main causes of our recurrent crisis and why it is becoming more of a husk of an idea than something of substance. Creation of personal imbalance, distraction from the self, stress due to shorter turnarounds, physical contact replaced with digital contact, an empathy gap due to mechanization of interactions, psychosomatic ailments, invasion of privacy, economic inequity, lot more political noise and polarization, ecological degeneration; the list of signals is endless.

Furthermore, along the way, the idea of innovation has become obfuscated. What was once an opportunity sponsored and seized by those inspired by it, has instead become a box-ticking exercise in service of survival. But innovation was never about plugging leaky holes in the hull of our present, it has always been about building that star-faring fleet of the future.

# 1.1  A World Shaped by Innovation

*Humankind is facing unprecedented revolutions, all our old stories are crumbling and no new story has so far emerged to replace them. How can we prepare ourselves and our children for a world of such unprecedented transformations and radical uncertainties?*

Noah Yuval Harar

I [Sujith] grew up in Kerala in South India in the 1970s. Back then, there were no smartphones, no computers, no landlines even. In my little town there was one landline phone, which luckily enough belonged to my grandmother.

Very often I would see neighbours queuing up to receive calls from relatives from further away than I could ever imagine. "How?" I used to wonder, "How on earth can these lines" - the connection for which had taken three years to apply for and receive - "...reach lands so far away?" But that's exactly what they did. Everyday there would be swarms of kids outside my grandmother's house undoubtedly thinking the same, waiting for the phone to ring so that they could watch the adults speak to their loved ones all across the country and abroad.

Yet, despite this wonderment felt by so many, landline penetration in the country remained slow, even though the demand for landline connections in India - a country that holds the idea of connection at its core - was extremely high.

Fast forward fifteen years later, and the dawn of the mobile phone erupted across the sub-continent. An entire generation of Indians missed landline telephony, meaning nearly a billion people. In a matter of years mobile telephones had connected the entire nation, from rich to poor, from the urban to the rural.

Innovation is integral to human evolution, and in a matter of decades it brought that wonder felt by those waiting outside of my grandmother's house into the pockets of almost every human being on the planet.

***

The world we live in today is the result of a long, winding stream of innovations which started when the first humans created tools to hunt and gather.

However, the speed with which our world is changing today is unlike any other. As we ride a technological wave charged by exponential growth, our experiences are being flung through uncertainty and chaos, further away from what we know and deeper into an existence which we are still unsure how to characterise. Like the arrival of the car or processing chip, a variety of technologies are now directing our societies and businesses in new directions, most of which we can barely imagine.

Looking back, the industrial revolution was a time of unprecedented change. Luciano Floridi, Oxford Professor of Philosophy and Ethics of Information and Director of the Digital Ethics Lab, in his book titled *The Fourth Revolution* examines how today differs from then: "The first revolution that changed our society, the agricultural one, took thousands of years to fully develop its effects; the industrial revolution needed centuries to do the same. This last revolution will take just a few decades".

Closer to now, we only need to look at the past 5o years to see that the impact of innovation has been radical. Over the course of the twentieth century, the world's population has quadrupled, with it doubling in the last

40 years alone. Out of that population, almost 1.1 billion fewer people are living in extreme poverty than in 1990 - despite a global recession - with life expectancy increasing by 20 years since 1960. A trip between London and New York took three and a half days in 1960[1], today it takes under eight hours. In our pockets we have more power and technology than the earlier space missions, one of which took us to the moon and back.

And these are only a few recent footnotes in a library of evidence that shows how innovation has rapidly shaped our world and improved our lives. The last revolution drastically shaped the ways in which education, business and society were run. And since then, it never showed any signs of slowing down.

As we write this manuscript, we are in the midst of the fourth industrial revolution, known more commonly as Industry 4.0. This is a situation where - as the World Economic Forum succinctly labelled in 2016 - "[...]developments in previously disjointed fields such as artificial intelligence and machine learning, robotics, nanotechnology, 3D printing and genetics and biotechnology" are all "[...]building on and amplifying one another". *The Future of Jobs* report highlights the intersectionality of our time and the massive impact it will have on jobs. Even if "overall job losses are predicted to be offset by job gains, there will be a significant shift in the quality, location, format and permanency of new roles". Arguably, it is during these periods of industry-intersectionality that new job opportunities arise,

---

[1] The first transatlantic flights started after WWII. Already in 1946 there were almost daily flights connecting the two sides of the Atlantic ocean in about 15 hours. But flying in the '50s and '60s was very expensive, so the most popular option to cross the ocean were boats called "Ocean liners". The fastest one was the SS United States, which was able to take almost 2000 people from London to New York in three days and a half. It was also the last ocean liner. The first commercial jet-powered planes began flying at the end of 1950s sending the ocean liners completely out of business in the '60s.

as new skillsets are required and new models of education created. In effect, the joining together of these disjointed fields act as the canary in the coal mine for the need of new ideas in society.

What all of the above means for us as a species is dramatic. We live on systems that rely on an individual's ability to produce and consume in order for our economies to function. Without this guarantee, it is uncertain what the future holds. Modern technologies are not only changing the ways in which we as individuals work together, but perhaps are even going to entirely remove the need for us as a species to work, shifting our society faster than ever before outside of war time.

If we look to the words of Charles A Beard - one of the most influential American historians of the first half of the 20th century - we might better understand one of the reasons why our volatile world is seemingly unsolvable: "Technology marches in seven-league boots from one ruthless, revolutionary conquest to another, tearing down old factories and industries, flinging up new processes with terrifying rapidity." One lesson we can take from this is that we as a species are renowned for our ability to automate processes – however once we automate each facet of every process, the question that remains is: "What is left for us?" Such a question elicits an understandable amount of worry, and only adds to the uncertainty that is characteristic of our time.

For now, we are but in the teething age of this automation process. Yet it rings true that we are living in a time dedicated and directed by technology. Three billion of the planet's eight billion people use social media, with an estimated 210 million people estimated to be suffering from either internet or social media addiction – approximately 55% of teens were more sleep deprived in America in 2015 than they were in 1991. On top of this, college students who went to college after the year 2000 are considered 40% less empathetic than those who came before them. Worse still, close to 800,000 people commit suicide every year – that's one every forty seconds.

Our worries about technology replacing humans are reasonable reactions to the current context and predicaments.

A new approach then is necessary, as technology is indeed transforming how we live, and our brains - a millennia in the making - are understandably not programmed for such rapid change. What this will do to a culture that is already hyper connected, we can only speculate. But if our context now is anything to go by, it will have consequences – and not all will be positive.

The internet for example, once idolised as the great connector, is increasingly the cause of us growing further apart. Worse still, those born into the internet generation are continuing to experience more mental health problems than we have ever witnessed prior to now. According to a study conducted for Common Sense Media in 2016, fifty per cent of the interviewed teens feel addicted to their mobile devices. Even more, 59%, according to their parents.

At the same time as all of this, our world is undergoing a period of rapid global warming, leading to cataclysmic events that are increasing in their frequency and furore year on year. The Syrian civil war, at the time of writing in its seventh year, was in part attributed to intense drought caused by the Earth's continued warming, and its effects are still being felt across Europe.

Technology is also charging the two binary tribes of globalisation and protectionism, splitting our consciousness in two and creating a dialogue that is founded on disagreement and disdain. An overburdened EU continues to struggle to stamp out the rising populism seen throughout its sphere of influence, as old models born out of a postwar mentality fail to reflect the context in which it finds itself. Its *configuration*, a recurring theme throughout this book, is increasingly distancing itself from what made it so perfect when it began. The whole world is reacting to issues in a patchwork fashion, with its institutions more and more disconnected from the energy that made them great solutions in the first place and suffering as a result.

There have been many defining moments in human history, moments where a transformation was inevitable yet full of uncertainty. In these moments we can only move forward knowing that there is no way back from it. Once the transformation happens, humanity itself is reshaped and a new system is born.

# Integration Moment

*Innovation really matters.*

Whether it is the focus on innovating systems, processes or ideas, innovation matters. The old stories that we have relied on in the past are no more relevant while new stories that reflect our future are yet to emerge.

The world is reacting to issues in patchwork fashion in spite of the great leaps in technology and connectivity we have seen in the past 50 years. All these, and many more, of what we are facing emphasizes that innovation matters.

However, innovation also brings along with it great challenges.

The internet for example, once idolised as the great connector, is increasingly the cause of us growing further apart. We feel increasingly disconnected and – studies show – increasingly unempathetic. The rapid pace of technology evolution and the hyper-connectivity we experience also increases sleeplessness and social media addiction.

## Self-enquiries:

- *If you look at all aspects of your life, would you say it is better now than 20 years ago?*
- *What impact did innovation have on your life/happiness/fulfilment?*
- *What makes innovation so important for your life/work?*

# 1.2 The Struggles of Innovation



We reside in a small and diverse world made up of more than seven billion human beings. The impact we make today is being magnified as more and more people are born on this planet. This, coupled with the fact that we are more connected than ever, means that people, things and ideas move around the world with an ease never seen before. And it keeps accelerating.

The world of tomorrow will be very different from the one of today.

This acceleration has manifested in cataclysmic ways for many people and institutions, who continue to strive to bring innovation to the forefront of their lives and activities, but who are faced with barriers unheard of only a decade ago.

These rapid changes are in part due to how innovation is an auto-catalytic process. Auto-catalytic in the sense that it is a process which speeds up with time as it is able to self-catalyse itself. The term, borrowed from chemistry, indicates a self-sustaining process in which at least one of the products from a reaction is one of the reactants used in the process itself.

Innovation has all the characteristics of an autocatalytic or self-sustained process. Every innovation is based on previous ones and creates the ground from which other and better innovations follow. Disruption then - that had in the past taken centuries to unfold - is now being compacted into a scale previously unheard of, and the truth is we are blind in how to cope with this accelerated change. Lessons can of course always be taken from the past, but our current state of affairs is so unique in many different ways that wisdom from elsewhere, it would seem, is necessary.

This may be one of the reasons behind the rise in the number of people who define themselves as 'spiritual seekers'. According to a study by the Pew Research Center, the share of people who identify themselves as spiritual and who feel a "deep sense of wonder about the universe" has increased dramatically over the past ten years. Almost paradoxically, this is particularly true for tech-savvy millennials. It would seem then that there is something missing in our approach today, a gap which we are grappling to fill in our search for answers in understanding the increasing rate of innovation.

The struggle to find effective alternatives to the current approach to innovation is even more evident if we restrict our observations to the scientific and technological sectors, where innovation has created the most remarkable results in the last decades.

Organisations that want to remain relevant have always made significant investments in innovation of systems and processes (for example, knowledge databases, market research, creative networks and design thinking). Unfortunately, research shows that the rates of return on investments in innovation is decreasing dramatically.

A Deloitte report laments over a 'decade of decline and transition' with internal rates of investment (IRR) crashing down from 10.1% in 2010 to 1.9% in 2019. This period also witnessed the forecasted peak sales per asset[2] more than halving since 2010 (from \$816 to \$407 million), while the average R&D cost increased by \$980 million. With all the money in the world thrown at innovation, it still is not working.

So what is happening?

The belief that "if you put the right people, with the right tools, in the right place at the right time, they will generate the ideas and sparkle the innovation process ", helps explain how organisations have invested most of their efforts in three key areas:

- *Systems*: through the creation of systems, structures and network, organizations accelerated the information flow, the diffusion of knowledge across boundaries, and enhanced communication between all the relevant stakeholders such as universities, research labs, individual innovators and global libraries.

- *Methodologies*: to exploit the potential of the systems, organizations and experts created methodologies and tools such as brainstorming sessions, design thinking, agile projects, rapid prototyping.

- *Innovators*: in this era of innovation heroes like Steve Jobs, Jeff Bezos and Elon Musk, organizations are competing to hire the best innovators and talents. They are acting on the belief that innovators are cut from a different cloth. Extensive studies have been conducted to identify the "Innovator's DNA" and understand what makes innovators different from the rest.

However, in spite of all these efforts, innovation is not keeping up

---

[2] Peak Sales are an important metric in the pharmaceutical industry. It refers to the highest Net Sales of the applicable Licensed Product achieved during any Calendar Year following the First Commercial Sale of such Licensed Product within each applicable country within the Territory.

with the growing complexity of the problems humanity is facing, and companies are now seeking the next wave of thinking for accelerating growth.

But the question now is why is innovation not keeping up? Is innovation finite? Are there but few people capable of the task? Are we approaching the end of human ingenuity? Have we reached the limits of human capability? Nine out of ten startups, the heralds of innovation, fail. According to *McKinsey Global Innovation Survey* only 6% of executives are satisfied with their innovation performance. Even the old failsafe Moore's Law, one of the key drivers of economic growth during the last half century, is dead, or at least on its last leg, according to a recent Stanford Study. The growth rate underlying Moore's Law[3] "should have increased by a factor of 18[...] Instead, it was remarkably stable. Put differently, because of declining research productivity, it is *around 18 times* harder today to generate the exponential growth behind Moore's Law than it was in 1971". So, have we reached the limit of our capacity for innovation?

The answer is no, innovation is not finite. But it does seem that organisations are struggling to keep up with the speed of change in the world. In the period between 1880 and 1940, numerous technological advances significantly improved income and quality of life of people; electricity, electric light, petrol engines, aeroplanes, telephone, plumbing in the home, machinery for agriculture, and many other things that have transformed everyday life and multiplied our collective well-being. The Internet, the iPhone and recent innovations have created a lot of stories, entertainment, intellectual stimulation and emotions, but regarding income, employment and GDP, they are not comparable to the innovative industries of the twentieth century. To give an example, today Google (a global

---

[3] Moore's Law refers to an observation made in 1965 by Gordon E. Moore, a co-founder of Intel. Moore postulated that the number of transistors on a microchip doubles every two years.

giant) employs 88,000 people; Fiat (a local company) in the late 1960s had 158,000 employees.

The same Stanford study found that, if we are to take the U.S. aggregate number as representative, research productivity falls by half every 13 years. "Put differently, just to sustain constant growth in GDP per person, the U.S. must double the amount of research effort searching for new ideas every 13 years to offset the increased difficulty of finding new ideas."

Although research efforts are costly, they are by far not the sole cause of the woes felt by organisations today. A recent survey of 270 corporate leaders showed that the more significant obstacles to innovation were a medley of other issues which money itself cannot remedy. Inability to act on signals crucial to the future of the business was cited by 42% of surveyants. Cultural issues, by 45%. Politics, turf wars, and a lack of alignment were being cited by 55% of respondents. Lack of budget came fourth in the survey.

It comes as no surprise then that the interventions that yielded significant results in the past, such as business process re-engineering, customer relationship management, brand building, supply chain innovations, cultural change programs, systems development, etc. are no longer having the same impact as they used to.

What this signal is the need for a change of mindset, a new paradigm in organizational thinking. Another survey showed that "84% said that the organisation's culture was critical to the success of change management, and 64% saw it as more critical than strategy or operating model." Organisations are already sensing a shift in how work works, and business leaders today are already beginning to understand that culture itself is a business strategy.

Yet, nothing is really changing. Even though businesses are becoming more and more aware of these problems, they are unable to solve them.

Knowing what to do is not the same as doing what we know. Studies have in fact shown that all organizational change interventions (including cultural change) have a dismal track record; 70% of all change attempts fail to deliver the desired outcomes. Although companies have begun to look for ways to change their culture, they are looking for new solutions through the lens of that same culture and mindset.

Individuals and organisations are still approaching innovation with a self-preservatory and competitive mindset. This mindset, dominant over the last decades, champions personal achievement and winning over anything else. When innovation is infused with competition, it becomes a continually accelerating process. The side effect of this acceleration, combined with rising costs, is that fewer entities (organisations, and even nations) have the resources to keep pushing forward, resulting in the vast majority of the world being left behind in the innovation journey. It should come then as no surprise that the global innovation index reveals that it is the same countries who top it time and time again.

Dinopoulos and Syropolous, in their work *Rent Protection as a Barrier to Innovation and Growth*, suggest that incumbent firms may shift to "defensive" R&D to protect their market position, and this could cause research productivity to decline. This is a problem for humanity — it shows a huge wealth of untapped potential and progress, that is decreasing by the day.

And this lack of progress is being felt by the people on the ground, with their perception being that innovation has not made their life any better. 41% of Americans say life is worse today than 50 years ago. Even more in Italy (50%), Greece (53%), Nigeria (54%), Kenya (53%), Venezuela (72%) and Mexico (68%). This is, in part, due to the fact that we as a global community – individuals themselves and, in turn, workers – have undergone a shift in consciousness from one of self-preservation to that of self-realisation. Many today value work not through titles and salaries but through the integral good it generates for themselves or the world at large.

Organisations, on the other hand, are measuring the world through a completely different set of metrics, metrics which disagree with those they are trying to connect with as a whole. As innovation is an auto-catalytic process - wherein the more we advance, the bigger the challenges are that we create - every now and then we need a certain kind of disruption to be able to shift to a new level. A paradigm shift in not just what we do, but in who we are is needed. Being different will inevitably make us do things differently. That is what will drive us to the next level.

All insights then point to something within and beyond *culture* and *mindset* as the area where all organisations should investigate and invest to unlock the next paradigm of innovation.

And therein lies the reason for publishing this work. Innovation is not running out, but is slowing down dramatically to the peril of many. After years of struggling to keep up with the increasing rate of change, we stand on a precipice of a wider societal and technological leap as new values and technologies influence how we do business.

At a time when we need more innovation than ever before, it is unavailable to many. It is, in short, dying, and we must therefore create innovative organisations, and innovators, in order to remedy this famine of thought. To do so we must completely reinvent the ways in which we approach innovation by identifying the roots of the failures of innovation bodies in how they are interacting with this strange new world.

But, at the root of all of this, we must reassess how we approach ourselves as individuals and how we as individuals form the basis of our human family. In order to grow, we must begin to look at innovation with a different level of awareness, something which is sourced inside-out, not outside in, and go a layer deeper than what others have analysed before.

Before we start our quest, let us take a moment to find a common ground, a shared definition of Innovation that we can use as a compass in our journey.

# Integration Moment

The autocatalytic nature of innovation is disrupting our lives and society in unprecedented ways. And we are blind in how to cope with this accelerated change. That has led us to looking everywhere for answers, even the most unlikely place, spirituality.

Organizations have upped their spending on R&D with ever-declining rates of return. Plus, the interventions that yielded significant results in the past are no longer having the same impact as they used to. This 'innovation stalemate' is calling for something new, a radical shift in mindset and understanding.

Whether we approach innovation defensively or competitively, the motivations are often self-serving, and can therefore never truly be innovative in the deliberate sense. This is a problem for humanity — it shows a huge wealth of untapped potential and progress, that is decreasing by the day. And this lack of progress is being felt by the people on the ground in the form of a constant decline in their quality of life.

This calls for a paradigm shift in awareness of not just what we do, but in who we are. Being different will inevitably drive us to do things differently. We will look at innovation with a different level of awareness, something which is sourced inside-out, not outside in, and go a layer deeper than what others have analysed before.

## Self-enquiries:

- *What role does innovation play in your profession/organisation/field?*
- *How much of your innovation potential do you think you are expressing?*
- *What is getting in the way of your innovation efforts?*

# 1.3 What is Innovation?


*All language proceeds as a system of navigation.*
*Named things are fixed points aligned or compared,*
*which allow the speaker to plot the next move*
Bruce Chatwin

What innovation today means for us as individuals, and more importantly, what that word means for humanity at large is a paramount point to make going forward.

As with most of the abstract concepts of life, there are countless definitions for innovation. The word 'innovation' itself has a fascinating story.

According to Professor Benoit Godin and the Institut National de la Recherche Scientifique, innovation has been given many different meanings over the course of history. For an extended period, the word even had a strongly negative connotation, it was the secularised term for heresy. Only after World War II, did people begin to use the word innovation for creative advances, giving back to the word a positive meaning. For Monsieur Godin et al, innovation is: "*a deliberate human change to something existing to create something new*".

This more modern expression highlights the necessity of a deliberate action making innovation different from evolution. It also clarifies that innovation starts from something existing differentiating it from "invention".

There is, though, something missing to make the definition compelling for the world in which we live. Something that can help us measure how much innovation is delivering the promise of bringing humanity forward. In his book, *The Little Black Book of Innovation*, Scott D. Anthony defines innovation as *"something different that has impact"*. This idea of impact is essential because it makes innovation tangible and measurable.

Inspired by both definitions, we have come up with a definition that we feel serves better in our quest for a new innovation paradigm.

> *Innovation is an intentional human-driven change from something existing to something new that results in an impact.*

Innovation must be *intentional*. Innovation does not happen on its own, it is not a natural occurrence in the same vein as biological evolution, for example. It is the result of a conscious decision to create something different from what we have now in response to our needs.

Which takes us to our second point. The fact that innovation is a conscious choice makes it inseparable from *human* intention. Innovation is an intrinsically human phenomenon, and arises out of our unique ability to envision something different to our current context, and seek out solutions with an awareness that is yet to be discovered elsewhere in our universe.

And our deliberate, uniquely human decisions to look for ways to improve ourselves suggests another trait of innovation; *change*. The word "innovation" comes from the latin *innovare,* "to renew, to change" from *in-* "into" and *novus* "new". If an idea does not facilitate change, then it cannot be seen as innovative. Today, there are huge debates about the difference between invention and innovation. For Schumpeter they are the first two parts of technological change in a free market. Invention is the conception of a new idea or process, and innovation consists of arranging the economic requirements for implementing an invention. In the common lexicon, the former is the creation of something new out of thin air while the latter is the change of something that exists. However, this distinction is driven by a human-centric view in which we value the "owner-ship" of ideas. As you will see later in this book, we - the authors - see ideation as a process of channelling and not of creation, so the distinction is not meaningful for the scope of this book. What is relevant is that inno-vation is about change.

For innovative change to occur, it must not merely follow what has come before. Instead, this change must be into something fresh and *new* if it is to be considered truly innovative. Imagination is therefore one of the main ingredients of innovation. To innovate, we must be able to make the invisible visible. We must be able to see beyond what exists to imagine what is possible...and bring it into our reality. Without newness, we are just improving something.

To innovate is also to have an *impact*. If something is created new - deliberately and with the foresight that it can change something - but it fails to do so though, then it cannot be attributed to the title of innovation. It must create a measurable impact and value. Without impact, it is simply a dream.

Armed with this comprehensive definition, we should be able to look more holistically at innovation and identify what lays beyond the current understanding of innovation.

# Integration Moment



We define innovation as an intentional human-driven change from something existing to something new that results in an impact.

To summarize, innovation is the result of a conscious decision to create something different from what we have now. It is an intrinsically human phenomenon. And, if an idea does not facilitate change, then it cannot be seen as innovative. Lastly, innovation must create a measurable impact and value.

The five attributes of innovation then, are:

1. *Intentional.* We take deliberate action, like making choices and acting towards innovation;
2. *Human-driven: Innovation is driven by us rather than happening to us;*
3. *Bearing change: An innovation changes the status quo;*
4. *Catalysing novelty: While an innovation changes the status quo, it also creates something novel;*
5. *Impactful: Innovation positively impacts the life of others.*

## Self-enquiries:

- *What is your definition of innovation?*
- *How do you relate to our definition of innovation?*
- *What does impact look like for you? How would you measure it?*
- *Looking at your field, what role will human contribution have in innovation?*

# Part II:

## Awareness Informs Configuration

In 1997, Professor Gary McPherson from the University of Melbourne decided to do an unconventional experiment to answer a simple question: "Why are some children quicker than others at learning an instrument?"

For his study, he randomly picked 157 children between seven and nine years old. For years he followed and monitored them, keeping track of their progress using biometric tests, recording their practice sessions, and doing a series of interviews.

During the first interview, even before the beginning of the first lesson, McPherson asked each child: "How long do you think you'll play your new instrument?" Based on the answers, the children were divided into three groups depending on the length of their commitment: short, medium and long term.

It was this particular question that proved to be most insightful. What surprised McPherson was that the students of the group who had foreseen a long-term commitment improved at speed four times higher than the children of the group who planned to engage only in the short term. Even if they were doing the same number of hours of practice with the same frequency.

There it was, the most decisive element in defining the speed of learning in the kids was not the IQ, or the sense of rhythm, or any particular motor skills. The defining element was the perception of themselves that each child had, even before starting to play any note. According to

McPherson's study, what was making some students better at learning an instrument was a voice within them saying "I'm a musician" instead of just "I'll learn to play an instrument".

In his book *Atomic Habits*, James Clear introduces a concept called the "Three Layers Of Behaviour Change" saying that "Outcomes are about what you get. Processes are about what you do. Identity is about what you believe." Every change involves all three layers in some ways - outcomes, processes and identity - but what really makes the difference, according to Clear's idea, is *the direction of change*.

The desire for change is usually triggered by the desire for different outcomes; we want - or we are asked to create - something different, so we begin a change process.

Where do we start from then? Because a change in outcome is the trigger, it is easy to begin the process by focusing on what we want to achieve (outcome-based interventions). Unfortunately, these kinds of interventions are short lived. Because our processes and our identity have not changed, we will quickly fall back into old ways.

In *The Little Black Book of Innovation*, Scott Anthony warns us about the mismanaged power of the "core "of any entity. He says that it "is a powerful magnet that can take the most powerful idea and turn it into something that has been done before." What he means by this is that, whatever great ideas we set out to implement, if the core of the individual or organisation does not change to support those ideas, it will deplete them of their transformative power. Like a magnet, it will keep us in known territories. This, as he calls it, is the 'sucking sound of the core'.

Smarter individuals and institutions quickly discover the limits of outcome-based interventions, so they intervene on their processes and systems (Processes-based interventions) to create better outcomes. With the help of experts and best practices, they implement new systems and procedures that are aimed at stimulating and sustaining new and better outcomes. This approach has been widely adopted in the last decades, thus creating outstanding results for many individuals, institutions and communities worldwide. Unfortunately, it works well in times when the "rules of the game" are stable and well-defined. As we saw in the previous chapter, this is no more the case for the VUCA[4] (volatile, uncertain, complex and ambiguous) world in which we all live and operate. In particular, when it comes to innovation, that is above all an act of change, we have seen many evidences that these interventions are struggling to provide the solutions to the challenges we are facing.

Then, as Clear suggests, the direction of change must go inside-out and it must begin from who we are, our identity as individuals, organizations or communities.

As we learnt from the research of Professor Gary McPherson, when our actions are an expression of our identity, of who we truly are, they are much more powerful and sustainable in the long term. Sustainable transformations that lead to exponential outcomes must then sprout from identity (Identity-based interventions); by focusing firstly on who we are and who we wish to become. From there it will be easier to allow the emergence of processes and behaviours that are in tune with our identity.

When it comes to innovation then, the above implies that we should design our own behaviour not to create innovation, nor to improve how we do innovation. We must begin by re-igniting the innate innovator who lies dormant within each one of us and is capable of boundless innovations. We call him/her the *Being Innovator*.

---

[4] "VUCA is an acronym – first used in 1987, drawing on the leadership theories of Warren Bennis and Burt Nanus – to describe or to reflect on the volatility, uncertainty, complexity and ambiguity of general conditions and situations." From Wikipedia

# 2.1 The Being Innovator



*Happy families are all alike; every unhappy family is unhappy in its own way.*

First sentence of Tolstoy's novel Anna Karenina

It would be easy to imagine that to re-ignite the Being innovator, all we have to do is to study the life of the remarkable ones, the ones who left a mark on the history of humanity. We need only to learn the practices, techniques, gambits, skills and strategies that made the remarkable ones successful, and use them, modelling ourselves after them.

However, we can all agree that whatever we learn from successful innovators, and no matter how well we repeat it, it will not guarantee that we will achieve the same results. Otherwise there should be plenty of Gandhis, Mandelas, Steve Jobs and Elon Musks changing our world. Yet, if we move beyond what they did and how they did it, and instead explore who they were and are, we can uncover some precious lessons on where we can begin our journey as innovators.

The Anna Karenina principle, based on the opening sentence of the eponymous novel by Tolstoy,  states that "a deficiency in any one of a number of factors dooms an endeavor to failure". That is why imitating successful innovators is not enough to transform you into one like them. There are so many different factors and things which must go into the right place that it is almost impossible to succeed.

One reason for this being that the ones who achieve great results do not always know how they did it. Certainly they did not plan their success in advance. We can only look back into their lives, connect the dots and extract the lessons. Even then, we might only grasp part of their drivers of success.

The second reason is that we are not these legendary innovators. And they are not us. It is of course useful to study the best innovators, but it must be with the awareness that we are not them, and we neither live nor operate in their context. In short, we must avoid the risk of mistaking the map for the territory.

"The map is not the territory" is a powerful metaphor coined by Alfred Korzybski to illustrate the differences between belief and reality, between an object and a representation of that object. Often, perhaps too often, we confuse maps with territories, our model of something with the thing itself.

A map, being a representation of reality, is finite and partial. Those characteristics are what make a map knowable and understandable by whoever reads it. The territory, on the contrary, is infinite and whole. We can never know it or understand it fully using our rational minds. That is why we need maps.

A territory can be experienced and lived even without a map. But reading a map is not enough to say we experienced the territory. It is the same with one's identity. All the books about our innovation heroes are maps. Some are very rich and detailed, but there is always something that transcends any map we may have.

So, if maps of successful innovators are not enough for us to become so, how do we re-ignite the Being Innovator within?

It was never a set of skills or capabilities which made the above-mentioned innovators legendary. Instead, it was a certain 'inner state' that made them so. An 'inner state' that we are all born with.

Think back to when we were toddlers. Everything was new and unknown. We had to learn everything, and create and invent our solutions for every challenge, because we could not rely on our existing knowledge or skills. Later, in our growth journey, most of us are taught to believe that we are not creative.

One of the most-watched TED talks is one from 2006 by the late Sir Ken Robinson, in which the educationalist spoke about how schools kill creativity. And his talk is not the only one saying so. In another famous TED session, Dr George Land explained how he and his team developed a test to help NASA identify the best candidates to become astronauts. The experiment aimed to measure the creativity of the potential astronauts, and the test was so simple that Dr. Land and his group decided to submit the test to 5 year old children to see how they performed.

98% of them passed the test. They tested the same group at five-year intervals, and the results were surprising. Only 30% of those same children passed the test when they were 10 years old, with that number decreasing to just 12% when they reached the age of 15, and plummeting down to 2% once they reached adulthood.

As we age, the world makes more sense to us. We become experts in our select fields, gathering a logical understanding of the complexity of our surroundings. At the same time, our experiences condition us, leading us to develop stories, beliefs, biases and assumptions that compound and eventually become our truth. This conditioning filters the massive flood of data flowing through our senses, helping us cope with and relate to the world without being overwhelmed and paralyzed by it.

Neuroscientist Manfred Zimmerman discovered that our capacity for perceiving information sits at around 11 million bits per second. However, he estimates that our conscious attention capacity sits at approximately 40 bits per second, which means that every second, 99.9996% of the information we sense through our eyes, ears, skin, mouth and taste goes unnoticed.

Our conditioning determines how we perceive reality, but in doing so, it also narrows the range of possibilities that we can see. There are plenty of opportunities around us, all the time, but too often we are blind to them due to our limiting beliefs and logical moulds narrowing our vision. As a result, the solutions and ideas that we come up with remain confined to the boundaries of our conditioning.

It is clear then that re-igniting the Being Innovator is not about adding new knowledge, skills or competencies. Not that it would not help to mimic the choices and actions of past and present successful innovators. That can yield results. You could even argue that mimicking innovators is essential to do innovation. However, because you can only mimic processes, the impact is limited by the conditioning of our identity.

Therefore, to unleash the Being Innovator, we must begin by deconstructing our conditioning.

*Unleashing the Being Innovator is a journey of subtraction.*

Subtraction is the stripping back of our learnt biases, the unlearning of our stories and assumptions, and the peeling back of the layers of beliefs to reveal the infinite potential for innovation that we hold within.

We are not talking only about individuals. Institutions, organisations and society too are asked to turn the look inwards and begin a journey of subtraction instead of addition of further skills, processes or norms if they really want to unleash their full innovation potential.

# 2.2 Configuration



> *Culture is deep, extensive, and stable. It cannot be taken lightly. If you do not manage culture, it will manage you—and you may not even be aware of the extent to which this is happening.*
>
> Edgar Schein

Dr. Edgar Schein, a former professor at the MIT Sloan School of Management, has made a notable mark on the field of organizational development across many areas, including career development, group process consulting, and, as we will explore here, organizational culture. Schein developed his organizational culture model in the 1980s and its structural framework for culture is divided in three layers: Artifacts, Espoused Values and Basic Underlying Assumptions.

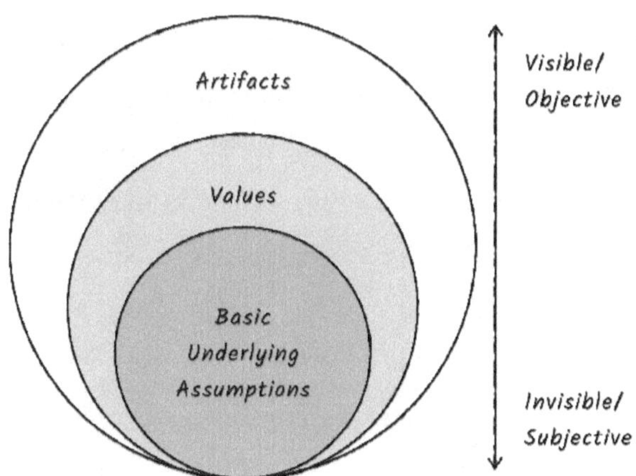

By *Artifacts and symbols*, Schein means the physical objects (furniture, tools, etc.), the physical environment (space, location, etc.) and the digital one (the cloud, communication platforms, shared working tools, etc.). And any other surface-level element visible to anyone who comes into contact with the organisation (such as the reception, the manifesto, informal or formal contacts between employees, way of working, etc.).

By *Espoused Values*, Schein refers to the deeper level of an organization's make-up that include its values and philosophy, and other drivers that inform its artefacts and symbols.

*Basic Underlying Assumptions* refer to the past experiences, challenges, successes, defeats, hopes and ambitions of those who founded and built the organization. These assumptions shape the core of the organization's culture and deeply influence the explicit values and the artifacts.

The content of an individual, the culture within an institution or the norms within a society are made of visible and invisible layers, all interdependent. So, any lasting and impactful transformation can happen  only when all layers are considered, as Schein argues, and also the direction of the transformation is an inside-out one.

For the purpose of this text, we call the combination of these visible and invisible layers, along with all the involved stakeholders and their systems and processes, the *configuration* of any entity. The place where you live, the people you have drawn into your life, the job you have, the kind of governance of your land or organization, the structure of the institutions around you, a product or service that you may have innovated, the communication process in your workplace, your beliefs systems and habits, and, in short, the life that you have created can all be referred to as configuration. Configuration is what separates one entity from another. It is what gives an individual, institution or society its unique form and shape within an environment.

In his book *Principles of Topological Psychology*, published in 1936, psychologist Kurt Lewin defined a simple yet powerful equation: *Behaviour is a function of the Person in his or her Environment, or B = f (P,E).*

Lewin's idea was that a person's behaviour, what she does and says, is always informed by both her identity - the characteristics determining who she is - and the environment in which she is operating. Widening the scope of Lewin's equation and taking into consideration what we shared before, we can rewrite it as: *A Configuration is the function of the Identity in its Environment, or C = f (I,E).*

The *configuration* that we, as individuals or collective entities, adopt is informed by the *environment* in which we operate and our *identity*. We adopt the configuration that better serves our identity in the environment.

With "environment" we refer to everything visible and invisible outside a configuration. We cannot directly change the environment, we can only adapt our configuration. And configuration being a function of identity, we must point our focus towards identity if we want to make significant transformations to our outcomes.

Instead, currently the typical approach to improve the innovation capability of any entity, be it individual or collective, is to analyse the configuration of that entity and use that finding to map a well-defined journey of learning and changing. And that, even if we know that the map is not the territory and that innovation is about moving into uncharted territories, ones which by definition have no maps whatsoever.

Literature and experts on innovation focus mainly on the study of successful configurations to extract models that can be replicated. The process typically goes as follow:

1. A new configuration emerges, one that creates a leap forward in innovation and gives a massive advantage to an entity.

2. The new configuration is then studied, modeled, improved and adopted by everyone, bringing followers up to speed. The ones

that do not adapt to the new winning configuration often disappear or become irrelevant.

3. This new wave of innovation makes the world accelerate at increased speed, to the point where the configuration cannot keep up with the pace of the new world it has contributed to create. A crisis period then ensues until a new configuration emerges and we go back to point 1 again.

This cycle has two problems. The first is that when we focus on configurations, we are easily made victims of Survival Bias[5]. We analyse configurations only after they have emerged and become visible. And often they become visible only after they succeed. It is easy to assume that the reason why an organisation or society is successful is due only to the configuration adopted. That is a limited vision because we do not see all the organisations or societies that failed using the same configuration.

The second issue is that, due to the increasing acceleration of the innovation process, the lifespan of successful configurations is shrinking. Hence, organisations are called to adapt and shift to new configurations more frequently. Unfortunately, that is easier said than done, which results in many organizations being left behind. This is even more visible on a global scale, with entire countries being left out of the innovation race as we noted in the previous chapter.

It is clear then that working on configuration is not enough and a different kind of leap is needed; one that requires for us to look beyond configurations and instead delve into Identity.

Unfortunately, when we focus on Identity we are presented with two

---

[5] Survival bias is a cognitive bias that leads us to focus our attention on the people or things that succeed in something while we overlook those that did not, typically because they are less visible or known. In doing this we have only a partial representation of reality from which we infer false conclusions.

major challenges. First is our inherent tendency to measure and model things, and the second is our inclination to dismiss subjectivity.

The visible layers of a configuration are the ones we know how to *measure* and *model,* so it comes as no surprise that change-makers, leaders and culture experts favour interventions mainly on these layers. Peter Drucker's maxim "What gets measured, gets managed"[6] is almost a *mantra* in the field of organization development.

Measurability is still the main criteria used to decide where to put our attention. As a result, studies have focused mainly on the visible layers, almost going as far as to suggest that the invisible ones, being not measurable, are not worth investing in. We already noted that this approach may have worked in the past, but it is not fit for the speed and uncertainty of the present and, even more so, the future. Unfortunately, despite a growing awareness among leaders that a shift in mindset is needed, there is resistance to embrace an alternate path due to the difficulty in measuring interventions.

The second obstacle in shifting our focus beyond configurations is the same scientific mindset that is at the very origin of the innovation results of the past two centuries. We can acquire knowledge through three distinct avenues: empirical observation, rational thought and introspection. Science, however, has taught us that we must stand clear of subjectivity if we

---

[6] The truth is that this famous quote has never been said or written by Drucker, who had a more nuanced perspective on measurement. In 1956, two years after the publication of *The Practice of Management* by Drucker, V. F. Ridgway wrote a paper titled *Dysfunctional consequences of performance measurements.* In it, Ridgway argues that the  indiscriminate use (of quantitative measures) may result in side effects and reactions outweighing the benefits." In short, as Simon Caulkin perfectly wrote in his article *The rule is simple: be careful what you measure* for The Guardian,  What gets measured gets managed - even when it's pointless to measure and manage it, and even if it harms the purpose of the organisation to do so." Unfortunately, only the first part of this sentence caught on.

are to find the truth. As a result, we put all our energy only into empirical observation and rational thought while we overlook, though not necessarily completely ignoring, the power of introspection. In the effort to create a culture of innovation within teams or ecosystems, people are asked to be objective even if that is clearly impossible. We cannot stop being human.

Consequently, the effort to be objective creates a resistance that depletes the power of the systems and processes we use to innovate. Plus, as we shared in chapter one, innovation is an "intentional human driven" change. Being human is paramount to being an innovator, yet too often it is seen as an obstacle instead of an opportunity. This is perhaps why 75% of adults believe that they are not living up to their creative potential.

In the end, we see the world not as it is, but as we are. What we call reality is our experience of it. Our assumptions and beliefs inform our experience of the world. They inform our systems and structures, how we manifest and relate to the world in which we operate.

Embracing subjectivity is then another hint about the direction in which a new paradigm for innovation can be found; beneath and beyond the layer of our configurations and identity, both visible or invisible. We are called to explore the knower in the knowing, the experiencer in the experience. The invitation is to look at the deeper layer that can unlock infinite potential for innovation; the *being* within the *doing*, the *self*.

However, *self* is an elusive concept. First of all, we need to embrace subjectivity and turn our attention inward, then we need to move beyond the models and measures we are used to rely upon; albeit them being incredibly valuable to understand configurations, they cannot tell us much about the underlying nature of *self*.

In order to unleash new levels of creativity and innovation, we need a new paradigm. One rooted in the science of awareness.

# Integration Moment

Unless our priority goes towards *being innovative* rather than simply *doing innovation*, we hamstring our potential and will be less likely to be successful in what we want to achieve, as Gary McPherson proved through his experiment decades ago. This implies shifting our focus from configuration-based intervention, where the focus is on outcomes and processes, to identity-based innovation.

Breakthrough innovations that lead to exponential outcomes sprout from interventions that tap into the realm of the *being*. This is true for the individual as it is for the collective.

Becoming a Being Innovator is a journey of subtraction, a subtraction of all our conditioning. This process is different from the often seen habit of blindly imitating successful innovators of the past or by embodying their configuration. After all, reading a map is not the same as experiencing the territory.

Two barriers hold back most professionals and organizations from innovating from the deeper layers. One is the need for innovators to measure and model, the second is the tendency of scientists to dismiss subjectivity. However, the deeper layers are human layers and hence are subjective by its very nature. They are just constructs built through our subjective experience of life. Hence dismissing subjectivity is prone to disqualifying the human experience, which limits breakthrough innovations.

In this work, we study the subtler layers within individuals and organizations that can unlock infinite potential for innovation, the *being* in all the *doing*. We explore *awareness*.

## Self-enquiries:

- *What do you believe to be necessary for innovation to be successful?*
- *How do you see yourself in the context of innovation? Would you call yourself an innovator?*
- *What do you feel makes your innovation heroes so successful? Which of their traits or characteristics do you see in yourself?*
- *What is hindering innovation in the culture of your organisation or environment?*

# 2.3 Awareness Informs Configuration


*Consciousness cannot be accounted for in physical terms. For consciousness is absolutely fundamental. It cannot be accounted for in terms of anything else.*
Erwin Schrödinger

On a Summer day in the early '90s, approximately 60 men, women and children sat in a college gymnasium, concentrating on not concentrating. These people, meditating in a side of a town known for its liberal use of guns and violence, were participants in an unconventional study that hoped to prove that transcendental meditation could in fact reduce crime.

The study, conducted by the Institute of Science, Technology and Public Policy (ISTPP), took place over two months and involved 4,000 participants. These participants, all practitioners of transcendental meditation, were littered throughout Washington D.C. and engaged in two daily meditation sessions lasting from two to four hours.

Mr. Prohs, chairman of the Long Island Capital of the Age of Enlightenment in Northport, told the New York Times at the time that meditation could reduce violence by creating "a powerful influence on the larger level of consciousness." Prohs believed that "...without going into your house personally, we can affect what goes on in your house." The idea being that a higher level of awareness would seep into the wider community.

What is going on at an individual level when meditating cannot of course be viewed by the naked eye. What can be seen however, is how the results of meditation manifest themselves in the physical world. In the last week of the study, when the control group of participant-practitioners was the largest, a whopping 23% decrease in violent crime was observed. Even when factoring other variables such as temperature, the researchers concluded that, over time, their study had led to a 48% reduction in violent crimes in the District of Columbia. Transcendental meditation then, was found to lead to a highly significant decrease in violent crimes.

What the ISTPP did was to focus on raising the collective 'awareness' of the community rather than focus on its manifestation. And by shifting the awareness of the group into subtler states, a tangible and measurable change manifested in the larger community.

***

The world in which we live in and the way in which we innovate, are mostly rooted in the idea that "matter is the only reality". A worldview known as *materialism*. It is a worldview based on a few key assumptions, the first of which is that matter is all that truly exists. Mind and consciousness then, are nothing but electrical and chemical processes between basic physical elements in the brain. In short, according to these beliefs, we are incredibly effective biophysical machines.

As we saw in the first part of this book, this paradigm has served humanity quite well so far. It has led to innovations that have been incredibly beneficial to the world. However, it has also created greater challenges, to which we now struggle to find an answer within that same paradigm.

Not only the most forward thinking scientists and visionaries, but also the contemporary mainstream feel that a radical shift is now needed. This need for a quantum leap is emerging from society and its institutions who feel that the existing paradigm on which innovation is rooted is unable to provide the breakthrough answers they are looking for. However, as the historian and philosopher of science Thomas Kuhn illustrated in his book, *The Structure of Scientific Revolutions*, we cannot evolve the existing paradigm by staying within its parameters.

Hence we are called to innovate also the paradigm, challenging its assumptions in order to open up the space for new breakthrough innovations to emerge. It has already happened in the past; recollect the copernican revolution[7] or the development of quantum mechanics in the first decades of the last century in the West.

Inspired by the spirit of exploration and experimentation that has guided all the great innovators of the past, we are called to step beyond our current beliefs and assumptions. For the new paradigm of innovation to emerge, we must move beyond the assumption that "matter is the only reality" and - using the words of Max Planck, a Nobel Prize-winning German physicist and the father of quantum theory - *"regard matter as derivative from consciousness."*[8]

We must recognise that awareness *(in this book we use awareness and consciousness interchangeably)* is the fundamental, underlying reality from which matter, in the most broader sense, is derived.

It is only by embracing an awareness-first perspective, as suggested

---

[7] "The Copernican Revolution was the paradigm shift from the Ptolemaic model of the heavens, which described the cosmos as having Earth stationary at the center of the universe, to the heliocentric model with the Sun at the center of the Solar System." from Wikipedia."

[8] "As a man who has devoted his whole life to the most clearheaded science, to the study of matter, I can tell you as a result of my research about the atoms this much: There is no matter as such! All matter originates and exists only by virtue of a force which brings the particles of an atom to vibration and holds this most minute solar system of the atom together. . . . We must assume behind this force the existence of a conscious and intelligent Mind. This Mind is the matrix of all matter." - Max Planck

by Plank, that we can move beyond the boundaries of existing configurations and unlock new levels of innovation.

What is awareness then?

Despite the effort and dedication of many scientists and mystics, awareness remains an elusive concept for most to grasp. One reason is that our reasoning and logical mind does not have the tools and words to comprehend something as formless as awareness.

Another reason is that often awareness is studied from the materialistic belief that matter is the only reality, so the focus goes to empirical observation and rational thinking. Empirical observation allows us to become aware of the patterns and behaviours of the reality we observe. To give you an example of how empirical observation works, when policymakers go about developing and releasing new legislation, they often begin with ordinances, a light version of the legislation envisioned. Once the ordinance is released, it is followed by observing how the sample constituents respond to the ordinance. This empirical observation informs the policymakers on the receptivity of the legislation among the larger constituents.

Thereafter, through rational thinking and deduction, we create templates and models that explain the patterns noticed through empirical observation. We use this faculty to analyse the findings from constituents, what works and what does not, and what further adaptations are to be made in making the legislation suitable for the context.

Rational thinking helps us understand how reality works and predict an approach suitable for its future. Yet still, we have no clues on that reality's underlying nature. We know how it behaves, not what it is. There are plenty of such models and frameworks defined over the last decades that we could have used as our map of awareness; Maslow's hierarchy of needs, Spiral Dynamics and Laloux's Teal Organizations are a few of the most popular, especially in contexts studying organisational behaviour.

Part II: Awareness Informs Configuration

Maslow's hierarchy of needs is one of the most enduring contributions to human motivational theory, combining the scientific with the philosophical in order to offer a more holistic understanding of human existence that includes awareness. Indeed, he provides a more holistic understanding of the world and even goes so far in his book *Motivation and Personality* (1954) as to state that holism is true and everything in the world is interrelated.

In the paper, *A Comparison of Maslow's Theory of Hierarchy of Needs with the Pancha Kosha Theory of Upanishads*, Anuradha Sathiyaseelan and Sathiyaseelan Balasundaram contrast Maslow's more holistic approach with the more reductionist philosophy of Skinner (1953), who views human behaviour as strictly determinable by one's environment. The authors point out that, as with many western attempts prior to Maslow, such ideas fail to cover the 'intangibles' in human behaviour and existence, and, viewed from a spiritual perspective, "all other Western theories fail to explain the cause or reason for human existence and man's constant effort to exceed himself."

So, it is clear for us that all these maps, albeit well-designed and extremely valuable on many levels, cannot help us in our quest into the realm of awareness. In short, this approach of combining empirical evidence and rational thought gives us an extensive understanding of how an entity operates internally and behaves externally, but such an approach tells us nothing about the entity's essence.

Therefore, to explore the realm of awareness we must be ready to follow a new route; one that embraces introspection to go beyond and beneath the 'how' and 'what' - what we know as objective experience - and instead unveils the subject of the experience itself, the *self.*

Again, this involves a journey of *subtraction.*

To steer clear of the influence of the material paradigm we decided to peel away the layers of knowledge and conditioning humanity has accumulated over the centuries and go back to the timeless wisdom of the sages. We have chosen in this manuscript to rely on the wisdom sourced from way before modern science. This wisdom, a body of ancient Sanskrit texts known as the *Upanishads*, were originally taught orally over thousands of years. Because of this, many of course have been lost to time, but 108 of these wise-old lessons are still known today.

Although Eastern in nature, many of the concepts of the *Upanishads* are shared in the West, with particular similarities found in the Platonic tradition. From the relation of mortals to gods, through to the idea of the *self* and even the use of the imagery of a charioteer struggling with two horses to describe our inner workings, although this knowledge may seem distant and far-flung, it truly reflects the complex human reality since its creation eons ago.

Even in modern times, these ancient ideas have found what one may think would be unlikely bedfellows. Erwin Schrödinger, the Nobel Prize-winning Austrian-Irish physicist who developed a number of fundamental results in quantum theory (and the man behind the famous Schrödinger's cat thought experiment[9]), was a staunch believer in the power of these oldened tomes: "In the whole world there is no study so beneficial and so elevating as that of the Upanishads. It has been the solace of my life. It will be the solace of my death."

Why would one of the grandfathers of quantum physics state such support? The answer lies in the nature of reality, and how, by the early

---

[9] The cat paradox, devised by Schrödinger in 1935, it's a thought experiment that illustrates an apparent paradox of quantum superposition. In this imaginary experiment, a hypothetical cat may be considered simultaneously both alive and dead as a result of being bound to a random subatomic event that may or may not occur. Schrodinger created this experiment as a teaching tool to show how quantum theory's misinterpretations can lead to absurd results.

1900s, physicists had begun to unravel our classical understanding of it. During this period, it was discovered that subatomic particles such as electrons were found to behave in ways previously thought impossible: particles could exist in two places simultaneously.

This new theory, which upended the ones preceding it, made outlandish predictions that, contrary to the science at the time, came true. This led to Schrodinger and others realising that the world we see is not reality itself but a projection onto our consciousness - a detail noted down in the *Upanishads* thousands of years before modern experiments.

Praise for the *Upanishads* permeates throughout the Western world. Henry David Thoreau noted how whenever he read any part of the *Vedas*[10] he "felt that some unearthly and unknown light illuminated" him. Leo Tolstoy used to read extracts from the Vedas and Upanishads from the *Vedic Magazine*. His interest in these ancient texts is clearly visible in *A Letter to a Hindu*, a correspondence he sent to the director of *Free Hindustan*, a journal advocating the end of British rule in India. A letter that became a great inspiration for Gandhi. These texts then, are widely understood to be one of the most concrete and comprehensive spiritual texts ever conceived.

The *Upanishads* identify awareness as an independent monistic principle and recognize that we all are awareness. Awareness is more than just a skill. It is more than knowledge or understanding. The *Upanishads* conclude that we do not possess awareness, we are awareness. By the simple

---

[10] The Vedas are the spiritual texts which inform the practice of Hinduism (also known as Sanatan Dharma meaning "Eternal Order" or "Eternal Path"). The term veda means "knowledge" in that they are thought to contain the fundamental knowledge relating to the underlying cause of, function of, and personal response to existence. They are considered among the oldest, if not the oldest, spiritual works in the world. Definition adapted from an article by Joshua J. Mark on the *World History Encyclopedia* website. More on https://www.ancient.eu/The_Vedas/

fact of having air in our lungs and life in our blood, we all are aware.

*We are awareness having a human experience*

Awareness is the foundational source of human values and motives, and depending on the level of awareness, our values and motives will differ.

With this understanding of awareness, let us further reinforce our understanding of configuration as laid out in the previous chapter, where we postulated that "Configuration is a function of Identity in its Environment" $[C = f(I,E)]$.

Knowing that identity is an expression of our awareness, the equation we shared previously could be rewritten as, *A Configuration is the function of Awareness in its Environment, or $C = f(A,E)$.*

What does this revised equation imply for innovation?

First and foremost, it implies that to open up the space for new layers of innovation, we must reverse the mindset behind the innovation processes we are used to. This requires a leap of faith.

Configuration is what we see and experience, hence it is easy to imagine that by changing the configuration of an entity we can sculpt a new awareness. The dominant mindset is that if we do everything right, say we build the right configuration - be it a happy marriage, an effective organization, a compelling profession, a trusting team - then the desired awareness will emerge.

That is how many entities approach innovation in the matter-first paradigm. They study the model and description of a successful configuration that has in the past yielded useful innovations. From there they create a checklist. With that checklist in mind they set out to work and apply all items in the checklist diligently. They create and implement the right selection of artifacts, processes, systems, values and so on, almost like alchemists combining all these ingredients together hoping that gold, a new awareness, capable of radical innovations, will emerge. As history tells us, on rare occasions this approach may work, however most often it creates fleeting results, tensions and conflicts.

A radical shift is required. For whilst before we thought that it was configuration which predetermines our Awareness, what has been the driving force behind most innovative realities — if not all — is, in fact, that it is awareness which informs configuration.

*Awareness informs configuration*

This is a paradigm shift in our understanding of existence. Once we are ready to embrace this paradigm shift, we are set to usher in a new wave of breakthrough innovations.

But how?

Again, the *Upanishads* not only show us the direction, they also provide us with a simple, holistic and timeless map. The *Upanishads* lay out in meticulous detail the 5 levels of consciousness along with the corresponding characteristics, all contained in a body of science called the *Pancha Koshas*[11]. For this treatise, we have gone straight to the source and adopted this science. The *Pancha Koshas*, or the five sheaths in Sanskrit, are considered to be channeled into this world by the ancient *Vedic*[12] sages more than 3500 years ago.

---

[11] The *Pancha Koshas* are discussed in the Brahmanandavalli Chapter of Taittiriya Upanishad which is a part of the Taittiriya Samhita of the Krishna Yajur Veda

[12] Sages of the Vedic science.

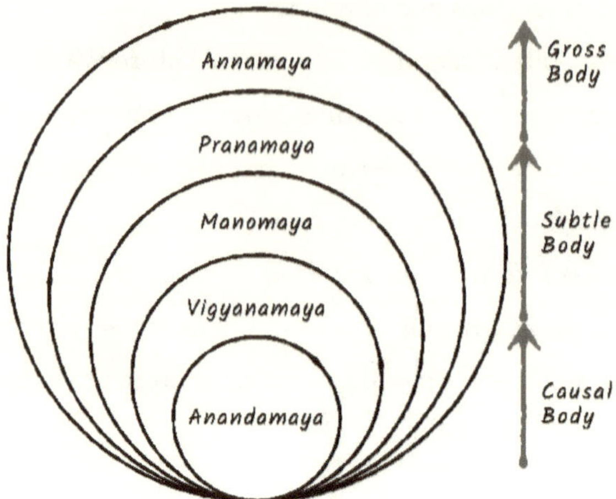



The science of *Pancha Koshas* recognizes us as multi-layered beings, varying from the Gross Body - which includes your flesh and bones - to the Subtle Body within - which includes the mind and vital energies - to the Causal Body further within - which includes the timeless and spaceless aspect of our being.

Contained within these 3 bodies are 5 layers that together constitute the *self*[13], viz. *Annamaya Kosha, Pranamaya Kosha, Manomaya Kosha, Vigyanamaya Kosha* and *Anandamaya Kosha*.

Associated with each of these 5 layers of awareness is a very unique creative potential. These layers can be easily thought of as layers of clothing, which divide the *causal awareness* from the materialistic reality of the world we experience through our mind and body, our configuration. All layers have different purposes and roles, with the outer layer being the most physically relevant one, and the innermost being the closest to pure awareness. Starting from the timeless and spaceless causal awareness and moving outward, each layer adds more substance to our being, adding new

---

[13] With *self*, we mean our manifested self or born self that differs from the notion of the self that refers to the soul or spirit in different wisdom traditions. Hereafter, whenever we use the word *self*, we will be referring to this born self.

faculties, characteristics and attributes.

The layer from which we operate in any given moment is contextual. Most of us are constantly floating between all the 5 layers depending on the circumstances. And from our material self, through a process of subtraction, each of the 5 layers can be unlocked so that their power can flow freely and manifest as breakthrough innovations in the world. More on this later.

The science of *Pancha Koshas* has three relevant benefits. They are;

1. *Simplicity:* It is a very simple model, one that does not require elaborate thinking to be understood. The way to leapfrog competition in a complex and uncertain environment is through simplicity. The kind of simplicity that allows children to thrive in uncertainty and unknowing. In the book, *Simple Rules: How to Thrive in a Complex World,* Kathleen Eisenhardt and Donald Sull state that "meeting complexity with complexity can create more confusion than it resolves." In a world that keeps getting more complex and uncertain every day - at the moment of writing we are amid a pandemic that has significantly raised the level of chaos - we need simple maps to spark action. Most modern models of consciousness result from empirical observation and brilliant thinking. As such, they reflect the variety and complexity of human configurations. The *Pancha Koshas* instead are an exercise in withdrawal that is *sourced,* rather than thought. In that lies its simplicity.

2. *Holistic in nature:* The *Pancha Koshas* apply to every individual and every ecosystem no matter the culture, religion, or historical context. Because the *Pancha Koshas* model is sourced from awareness and not conceived by analyzing configurations, it is not conditioned by the environment. Its essence is the same, no matter the configuration - individual, team, organization, community - or the

environment. Being as flexible as they are, the *Pancha Koshas* allow for a much more holistic mapping of any situation.

3. *Timeless/Evergreen*: Since the time of its divine conception (the a-ha moment), when it was channelled into this world (we will talk about the transcendent mind later), it has applied consistently to every known situation, and it has provided a clear map for a human's journey of awareness. The fact that it is still so influential to so many on the planet is a testament to this day. The *Pancha Koshas* are not a reaction to certain times because, in their ancientness, they are beyond the times.

In the following five chapters, we will lay out in great detail each of the *Pancha Koshas.* We will start this journey at the innermost layer of the *self,* the *Anandamaya Kosha,* and move outwards, following the direction through which awareness manifests into form. This route will demonstrate to you how we evolve from pure awareness into configuration and how we can unlock our potential for boundless innovation

Each layer holds one key to breakthrough innovations, and should we miss harnessing the power of any one of these five layers, the resulting innovation will be vastly reduced in its impact.

# Integration Moment

The next breakthrough in innovation will be created by the individuals and organisations that are able to harness their awareness. To do so, we must be willing to challenge the mainstream materialistic paradigm and embrace an awareness-first perspective. This means to accept that we are awareness having a human experience.

We do not have awareness, we are awareness. Awareness is not a characteristic of an entity, every entity is a manifestation of awareness.

There are plenty of systems and frameworks defined in the last few decades that we could have used in this book as a map for awareness. However, these systems and frameworks fail to cover the 'intangibles' in human behaviour and existence.

Hence we have built this treatise based on the ancient science known as the *Upanishads*. Even in modern times, these ancient ideas have found unlikely bedfellows. The *Upanishads* lay out in meticulous detail the 5 levels of consciousness along with the corresponding characteristics, all contained in a body of science called the *Pancha Koshas*, or the five sheaths in Sanskrit.

The science of *Pancha Koshas* recognize us as multi-layered beings, varying from the Gross Body - which includes your flesh and bones, to the Subtle Body - which includes the mind and vital energies, to the Causal Body - which includes the timeless and spaceless aspect of our being. Contained within these 3 bodies are 5 layers that together constitute the *self*. Corresponding to each of these 5 layers are certain awareness and intelligences. All layers have different purposes and roles, with the outer layer being the most physically relevant and the innermost, the closer to pure awareness.

The science of *Pancha Koshas* has three important benefits; it is simple, holistic in nature and is timeless.

## Self-enquiries:

* *Have you considered who you are beyond your body, emotions and thoughts? Is there a controller or observer of all your faculties?*
* *Identify a framework on which you can plot the maturity of an individual or group. What insights do you gain out of this exercise?*
* *The time when you had epiphanies, did you feel an outside force working through you?*

# 2.4 *Anandamaya Kosha* - The Violet Layer



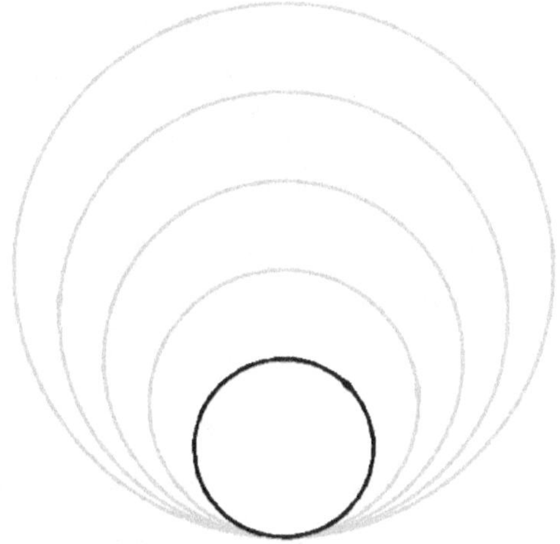

Carlos Santana needs no introduction. With 10 Grammy Awards and over 100 million albums sold worldwide, he is a music legend. From humble beginnings forged in the border towns of Northern Mexico, Santana has seemingly drawn from an endless well of creativity with a career spanning over half a century.

His name appears in every list of the best guitar players and he has been an inspiration to generations of musicians and bands. When talking of his music, the expression "universal tone" is often used to acknowledge the fact that by just hearing one note it is possible to tell that it is a Santana song. But there is more in this expression. There is also the recognition that for Santana, music and soul are interconnected.

In a 2015 interview with Las Vegas Magazine, he said that "Music gives a spiritual sense of order to the molecules in your brain and your lungs and your heart. Music reminds you of the forgotten song inside you." He went on to say that "Spirituality is something very tangible to give you assurance and a guarantee that the universe is abundant and at your service, but you have to learn how to access it."

The presence of spirituality in his songs is felt in both the old Santana and the new. From the sensual sounds of his band's cover of Willie Bobo's *Evil Ways* in 1969 to the furious guitar solos on *Shape Shifter* (2012), there is a level of forever being somewhere beyond the pale when it comes to Santana, a place of wild energy and drive.

Indeed, in a lengthy interview with Rolling Stone magazine in March 2000, Santana would talk of the influence of both angels and devils in his work. Both were crucial in connecting with what he called the "spiritual radio", in bringing balance to his work and to himself, "I have more of a balance now with the divine and the human, and I can dance with all of it now. That's probably why *Supernatural* is so powerful, because now it's not in conflict," Santana explains.

From 1972 to 1981, Santana took the name *Devadip* after he became a disciple of an Indian master called Sri Chinmoy. This is where his interest in spirituality and balance really took off; "You know, the halo and the horns are the same things. I mean, it's OK to be spiritually horny – that's what creative genius is really about."

Santana's understanding of the gods percolates throughout the interview, and that speaking to them is crucial to his work. "My reality is that God speaks to you every day. There's an inner voice, and when you hear it, you get a little tingle in your medulla oblongata at the back of your neck, a little shiver, and at two o'clock in the morning, everything's really quiet and you meditate and you got the candles, you got the incense and you've been chanting, and all of a sudden you hear this voice: Write this down. It is just an inner voice, and you trust it. That voice will never take you to the desert." By connecting to that cosmic other, he is able to bring change into his reality.

***

Santana is not alone in his description of being in the creative zone. Throughout culture, we understand the concept of 'getting into the flow'. What this is is actually our minds expanding into the innermost sheath of the *Pancha Koshas*, the *Anandamaya Kosha* or the Violet layer.

The word *Ananda* in *Anandamaya Kosha* stems from *aa* which means "all", and *nanda* which means "joy", with the sum of its two parts meaning "joy from all sides", or to borrow more modern terminology, a state of bliss. This layer is the first step in a human's birthing in which pure awareness manifests into a standalone form.

What is characteristic of this layer is that you have a form, but you do not identify with it. When we transcend into this layer, there is no relationship to the physical realm, only to the metaphysical reality. We are timeless and spaceless.

When we operate from here, all there is, is pure awareness. In the words of the masters, we are *Sacchidānanda*[14]; we are fully aware of Truth, we are aware of awareness and we are in bliss.

This transcended state - the *Anandamaya Kosha* or the Violet layer -

---

[14] *Satchitananda* (Sanskrit: सच्चिदानन्द) is a compounded Sanskrit word consisting of "sat", "chit" and "ananda", all three considered as inseparable from the nature of ultimate reality called Brahman in Hinduism. sat (सत्) in Sanskrit sat means "being, existence, truth", chit (चित्) means "consciousness" and ānanda (आनन्द) means "happiness, joy, bliss".

is where we access the faculty of Spiritual Intelligence, the faculty that allows us to experience unity or non-duality with ourselves and with others.

Spiritual Intelligence is the active ingredient of two functions essential to boundless innovation. The first function is *transcendence*. Transcendence is a state of being that is beyond time and space.

In our wakeful state, we operate in the object-oriented world. In this world, time is linear in nature, wherein there is past, present and future. A set of thoughts called memories are organized as events already experienced, whereas a set of thoughts called imagination or fantasies are organized as events yet to be experienced.

Similarly, space, in the sense of matter, is organized in three dimensions where objects and events have relative position and direction. It is finite and object-oriented, and can be experienced using our five senses.

When we go beyond the finiteness of time and space, we enter a strong subjective experience of the divine. In this state of peak experience, you no more identify with the *self*, you are overcome by the feeling of euphoria, time comes to standstill, and you are left with a profound sense of oneness with others, your environment, God, etc.

We have all experienced transcendence. Santana, in playing his music; children, in their play; lovers, in their love-making; devotees, in their devotion to the Supreme; sculptors, in their act of sculpting... — transcendence is not a faraway state for humans. Performers such as athletes and artists often explore how to increase their likelihood of getting into this transcended state. They work on themselves and on their environment, to create the conditions that ease them into this state. It is the experience that American-Hungarian psychologist Mihaly Csikszentmihalyi defined as *flow*; "a state in which people are so involved in an activity that nothing else seems to matter; the experience is so enjoyable that people will continue to do it even at great cost, for the sheer sake of doing it."

Part II: Awareness Informs Configuration

Time, when experienced in the state of transcendence, acts differently. When you are deeply absorbed in solving a problem, or developing a theory, or reading an engaging novel, or painting, or playing music, you experience this altered reality of time (or the feeling of timelessness). In that act, we transcend the worldly plane and enter that zone of timelessness that corresponds with the Violet layer.

Space too, when experienced in the state of transcendence, becomes infinite. In a spontaneous moment of spacelessness, you feel the presence of a dear one who is living across the globe, or two unrelated people have the same emotion about something.

Attesting to the fact of spacelessness associated with the Violet layer, multiple independent discoveries have happened on different ends of the earth, that too simultaneously, without apparent connection to each other, gives us a glimpse of the opportunities that can be unlocked when we enter this layer.

Such occurrences are more often than you think. In 2015, the Nobel Prize in Physics was shared by Takaaki Kajita of Japan and Arthur B. McDonald of Canada, who independently proved that neutrinos have mass.

In 1879, when Thomas Edison invented the light bulb, many others had already independently built at least 23 prototype light bulbs. Two different patents for the telephone were filed the same day by Alexander Graham Bell and Elisha Gray. Newton and Leibnitz simultaneously invented calculus. These are just a few examples of a vast phenomenon called "multiple discovery" or "simultaneous invention".

Another Hungarian Geometrist Farkas Bolyai said to his son János Bolyai, that "When the time is ripe for certain things, these things appear in different places in the manner of violets coming to light in early spring" in a bid to urge him to claim the invention of non-Euclidean geometry without delay.

Spiritual Intelligence is also the active ingredient of *intentioning*, the second of the two functions essential for boundless innovation.

*Intentioning* is not meant as a conscious process of *setting intentions*, but as an unconscious process of *being intended upon*. For example, you are not making a decision of what problem to solve, what solutions to develop or what features to build into a product. Instead, *intentioning* is one where, through a process of transcendence, from a deeper place, you receive the knowledge of a holistic problem that you are ordained to solve, or channel a paradigm-shifting solution that you are destined to source for the sake of humanity and the planet.

This experience of creating from pure awareness has been called many different names within different traditions over the course of time. Modern psychology sees it as something emerging from the inner psyche or the unconscious mind. Scientists might refer to it as connecting to genetic memory. Mystics recognize it as *intentioning*... experiencing the "divine spark". For many like Santana, *intentioning* takes the form of a 'higher voice'.

Such differences in language do not omit the similarities in meaning; creativity beyond the capabilities of our human form. A sense of awakening, presence and connection to all; this is the experience of the infinite potential of Spiritual Intelligence.

When we think of human intelligence, we usually locate it somewhere within the body, or at least at its boundaries. A characteristic of an entity separated from all the others.

Spiritual Intelligence allows us to dissolve that separation so the wisdom of the whole can flow through us. Those who transcend into the Violet layer can access Spiritual Intelligence and can engage with the mystical force of this layer. In doing so, we can *intention*, accessing a new realm of opportunities, invisible to others. All knowledge is already there in that realm for us to pick, like apples from a tree. When an individual or group transcends the material plane and operates from the Violet layer, they are best equipped to tap into that library of infinite knowledge, unrestrained by configurations which keep their access to creativity limited to the local mind. We empower ourselves as individuals or organisations, but also, as we saw earlier, we impact the world at large, thus taking our contribution to a whole new level.

Connection and wholeness beyond the self is typical when we are operating from this layer. We experience a sense of destiny, a quiet realization that "I am being who I am meant to be".

In 2010, researchers at St. Bonaventure University found that social flow experiences were reported as being more enjoyable than solitary flow.

Athletes describe the same feeling as being in the zone. Bill Russell, a key player for the Boston Celtics during the period when they won 11 professional-basketball championships in 13 years, put it thus; "Every so often a Celtic game would heat up so that it would become more than a physical or even mental game, and would be magical. That feeling is difficult to describe, and I certainly never talked about it when I was playing. When it happened I could feel my play rise to a new level... At that special level all sorts of odd things happened....It was almost as if we were playing in slow motion. During those spells I could almost sense how the next play would develop and where the next shot would be taken. Even before the other team brought the ball in bounds, I could feel it so keenly that I'd want to shout to my teammates, 'It's coming there!'—except that I knew everything would change if I did. My premonitions would be consistently correct, and I always felt then that I not only knew all the Celtics by heart but all the opposing players, and that they all knew me. There have been many times in my career when I felt moved or joyful, but these were the moments when I had chills pulsing up and down my spine."

As the word *flow* suggests, when we operate from the Violet layer we become a channel through which the infinite potential of awareness can manifest into the world. What we are capable of delivering in that state of transcendence is *peak performance*, the kind of performance that looks unreal to others.

It is important to reiterate that we must not unleash our Spiritual Intelligence and practice *transcendence* and *intentioning* with the ambition of harvesting innovations. When we unleash Spiritual Intelligence, it should not be about doing or achieving something. It should be about fully realizing who we are, our very unique potential. We must practice transcendence for the experience of exultation that comes with transcendence. Boundless innovations will naturally follow from there.

The next question is, how do we unlock the Violet layer? Or, more correctly, seeing as this layer is the first formed in the process of manifesting ourselves as entities in the material world, how do we reconnect with this potential that is already within us?

*Through subtraction.*

We can operate out of our conditioned self, with all its instinctive, sentimental and cerebral faculties, or we can access that timeless spaceless self that is already contained deep within our layers of conditioning.

Accessing that timeless spaceless self involves subtraction.

But how?

The answer can be found in the informed and diligent practice of meditation and mindfulness, and the relentless practice of love and beauty[15].

Meditation and mindfulness help us go beyond our wakeful self to the deeper realms of the thought-free self. Imagine peeling an onion. At the

---

[15] This dissolution of separation is known at the human level as love in relation to others and beauty in relation to objects." Spira, R., Kastrup, B., & Md, C. D. (2017). *The Nature of Consciousness: Essays on the Unity of Mind and Matter* (1st ed.). Sahaja.

core you arrive at space, an expansiveness that is formless, yet full of potential. Each peel of the onion can be seen as a layer of conditioning, be it our belief systems, habits or reflexes built through a lifetime of experiences.

Through a practice of focusing on being aware of the thoughts, sensations and feelings in the moment, without interpretation or judgment, you peel the layers of your belief systems, habits or reflexes. By deliberately unbounding the mind, you arrive at a blissful place that is known to be accessible to the likes of sages, children, or exceptionally self-authored individuals like the most creative scientists.

Through practicing love and beauty in everything we do, individually and collectively, we raise our energy and liberate our bigger self. Just think of all the heroes we celebrate, the big ones and the almost invisible ones, they all have in common an incredible love for what they do that makes them willing to sacrifice their smaller self to realise the purpose of their bigger self. Or artists who, in their relentless pursuit of beauty, were able to expand beyond their human limitations and create something timeless.

The key then is to create an environment around us and a set of practices that nurture love and beauty in everything we do and say. Such an environment is one with high levels of self-leadership and autonomy, with the reassurance that there is a deep sense of calling, so we feel invited to bring all of ourselves to serve the collective purpose.

Individuals, groups and movements which are steeped in the Violet layer are characterized by a sense of genuine joy. There is no attachment to outcome in this judgment-free environment, yet there is a natural passion for one's own efforts. Actions are noble and unconditional, and are seen as a means to self-realization. Compassion flows freely, with all parties experiencing intense synchronicity in the belief that their work is a service.

Mystical in approach, these unicorns allow play, foster allowing, and live humility. They view adversity as nothing more or less than anything else the world has created. This gives them the ability to see everything as an opportunity to create something new, and when times will require, such individuals, groups and movements will get into a state of flow, producing peak performance and breakthrough innovations that will have a transformational impact on society.

Breakthrough innovations, though, need us to take that which we have *intentioned*, into the next level of materialization. That implies harvesting the illuminations we receive when in a transcended state.

In Santana's experience, when "there's an inner voice, and when you hear it, you get a little tingle in your medulla oblongata at the back of your neck, a little shiver", there is an illumination awaiting. "Write this down," he says. "It is just an inner voice, and you trust it." This next step of taking the "divine spark" into something more real is the topic of the following chapter.

# 2.5 *Vigyanamaya Kosha* - The Blue Layer



*A child has no trouble believing the unbelievable, nor does the genius or the madman. It's only you and I, with our big brains and our tiny hearts, who doubt and overthink and hesitate.*

Steven Pressfield

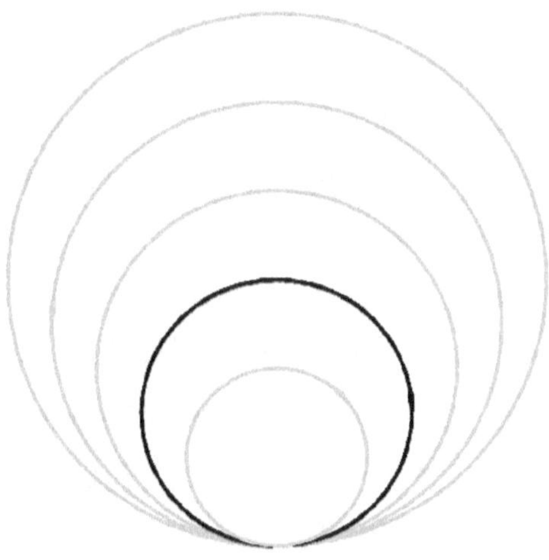

In his book *Creativity Inc.*, Ed Catmull talks about how he went from being an incredibly talented engineer to becoming the leader of one of the most successful companies of the time in the world, Pixar.

The most fascinating aspect is that he achieved his remarkable results - leading thousands of people, managing billions of dollars, and dealing with the complexities of a giant like Disney - with zero or little specific background in management.

One of the secrets of his incredible success was in fact not knowing how to be a manager or a leader. Because Catmull did not know what was right or wrong, what works and what does not, what was possible and what was not from previous studies or experiences, he had to create his unique way forward. With the innocence and curiosity of a child, he had to make sense of everything that was happening. Mostly through experimentation and intuition. With the courage of an explorer, he had to take the plunge into what was, for him, uncharted territory.

Indeed, such ingenuity and curiosity came at a cost, with Catmull going to work every day "feeling like something of a fraud" at the beginning of his career, owing to the fact that he did not share the more aggressive and classical leadership tendencies of other leaders.

This would last for some time, yet was part of a process that would eventually lead to a masterful take on how to run a company. It was not about pretending to understand how to run a company, instead the key to his successful management lay in the opposite, in not understanding management, and particularly in the ability to admit such shortcomings.

In his book, Catmull notes that: "I believe the best managers acknowledge and make room for what they do not know—not just because humility is a virtue but because until one adopts that mindset, the most striking breakthroughs cannot occur." This mindset, one that embraces the unknown with open arms rather than reacting to it with fear, was what would see Catmull overcome his imposter feeling and flourish.

"Managers," Catmull would go on to explain, "must accept risk; they must trust the people they work with and strive to clear the path for them; and always, they must pay attention to and engage with anything that creates fear. Moreover, successful leaders embrace the reality that their models may be wrong or incomplete. Only when we admit what we don't know can we ever hope to learn it."

***

It seems that Catmull understood what Aristotle said all those years ago, "The more you know, the more you realize you don't know." And instead of becoming frustrated by his own inabilities, he sought to know that which is contained in the unknowing.

Catmull's story is not so different from the ones of many other innovation heroes. They did not colour within the lines of what was known and possible, because they did not know or see those lines. They followed their intuition.

In the *Pancha Koshas*, the *Vigyanamaya Kosha* - the Blue layer - is a step forward in the manifestation of awareness in the material realm. It is considered the sheath of wisdom, intuition and creativity.

When in the Blue layer, we feel that there is more to us than what our limited minds can perceive or define. We experience spontaneous bursts of insights, a sudden dawn of *illumination,* or a random "a-ha" or eureka moment... all of which is a consequence of transcendence, a virtue of the Violet layer. These *illuminations* are the faculty of Intuitive Intelligence expressing itself, the intelligence native to the Blue layer. This intelligence allows us to see and perceive beyond the boundaries of our acquired knowledge and our cognitive understanding of reality.

Intuition is an elusive concept to explain by means of logic and reasoning. That is why in everyday language, intuition is placed anywhere but in the mind. We usually locate intuition in the body using expressions such as "gut feeling" or "feeling in our bones". Plato described it as a pre-existing knowledge residing in the "soul of eternity", and for Descartes, this pre-existing knowledge is gained through rational reasoning or contemplation.

We resonate with the definition that Paulo Coelho gives in his book, The Alchemist; "intuition is really a sudden immersion of the soul into the universal current of life, where the histories of all people are connected, and we are able to know everything, because it's all written there."

When we operate from the Blue layer, we are more in tune with our surroundings, capable of reading omens and sensing what is happening around us. By no coincidence, this is also exactly how children operate.

Toddlers for instance can sense into the reality of what is happening around them; if their parents are not in a good mood or if their siblings are in pain (or are faking it), for example. Such an ability is available to them from an early age and, with no previous reference, they are able to sense all of these things and act accordingly using the physical and cognitive faculties they have at their disposal, such as crying out loud.

And can you think of anyone more creative and innovative than a child in play? A child can transform every object in a new game, any space into a new world. To a toddler, this world made of and by adults must look so volatile, uncertain, complex and ambiguous (the famous VUCA world). With short and unstable feet, small hands, and limited knowledge, every-thing must seem so complicated to toddlers. Yet still they thrive.

Which then begs the question, what makes children creative? How can we revert to this state of creativity?

In *A Riot of Divergent Thinking*, executive editor of the British Medical Journal Kamran Abbasi details the importance of divergent thinking – the ability to interpret a question in many different ways and the ability to see many different answers to a question. However, Dr George Land's experiment that we shared before proves that our capacities for divergent thinking deteriorate with age. Massively, if we consider that 98% of the kindergarten children showed genius level in divergent thinking, while the percentage dropped to 2% once they became adults.

So what happened? Philipe Rochat details in *Five levels of self-aware-ness as they unfold early in life*, that we undergo a transformation of self-awareness throughout our childhood. Citing the poet Arthur Rimbaud who claimed that "I is someone Else" ("Je est quelqu'un d'autre"), Rochat writes that we conceive ourselves through the eyes of others. Nowhere is this more evident than in the transformation of a child around the age of 2-3 years, wherein they begin to display behaviours such as embarrassment or pride as a direct result of having others in mind when they act out their actions.

As we age, education, and in particular a "conveyor belt" education, which only champions the existence of one answer - right or wrong - takes this self-awareness to the next level. We may feel that our behaviours will be unrewarded, fail to please others, or may embarrass us due to failed reasoning. At this stage, already we see a disconnect from our limitless potential.

A child is a being at one with blue-sky[16] thinking. Yet, the utter focus on efficiency and productivity since the early school years crushes the natural curiosity and imaginative power of kids to be replaced with focus, structure and good behaviours.

To activate the potential of the Blue layer then is simply going back to the unconditioned awareness of childhood. Only then, we can unlock the bigger "*who*", the "self beyond the self" that we so often recognise in artists.

It is often a surprise when we meet, in person or through biographies, the men or women within remarkable artists or innovators. We are often left perplexed, asking ourselves, "How can this person be the same one who created such beautiful and inspiring art? Or innovation?"

---

[16] Blue-sky thinking is an open-minded thinking that is not grounded with or bound by the realities of the present. The origin of this expression is unclear. For some it suggests the emptiness of the skies and so the freedom from boundaries. Others see it as a reference to casual contemplation, like when you lie on your back pondering and watching the sky. The expression  blue sky and hot air" was used to describe the early 20th century practice in finance to sell things grounded on nothing tangible, from there possibly the concept of  blue-sky thinking" as something with no basis in reality.

# SUBTRACTION

On the surface, the person within and the artist may seem incongruent with each other. However, if we look a bit deeper, we can see that human beings have the potential to do things that are bigger than themselves. Things that go beyond the capabilities and limitations of their human form. This ability is more evident in artists, but it is innate in everyone. Again, children are the living proof of that.

We are all born with a natural ability to sense the whole through our intuition. Unfortunately, as we grow up, due to our conditioning and our environment, while we get better at sense-making, we separate ourselves from the whole, silencing our ability to sense through intuition. We begin to perceive ourselves as standalone entities, separate from each other, and we experience the duality of the world even if we cannot understand it yet.

That is why, as much as it is natural for a child, unleashing the potential of intuition can be really challenging for adults, on many levels. When the space shuttle breaks free of earth's gravity and gets out of the planet's atmosphere, it crosses a threshold. From that moment of crossing, everything is different. Going back is no more an option, not an easy one at least, and the astronauts have to deal with a whole new set of challenges. What they know is not enough, like how to move in the absence of gravity, so they must access their natural creativity.

For toddlers, such a threshold does not exist. They know so little about everything around them that they continuously use their intuition to sense their way forward. Whereas for adults, growing up we harden our boundaries through our beliefs and what we have learned, hence crossing that threshold becomes more and more challenging. Therefore, we must release our beliefs and unlearn what we have learned if we are to be as intuitive as children are and become a fountain of illuminations.

When we embrace a kidful state, we see the world through the eyes of our intuition, unbounded by the conditioning we have acquired and built overtime. It is a kind of creative superpower, one that is not easy to deal with.

Not so for children.

Take some time to observe any child in your life and you will notice;

- They shape the world around them by ignoring what they do not want. Unwanted things just become invisible to them.
- They approach everything with a playful mindset. Everything is a game.
- They are not bound by reality, so they easily bend it to accommodate their visions and desires.
- They take what they want or, if they cannot, they are clear - and often loud - in expressing their desires.
- For them, everything is possible until proven not possible. Even then, they will stretch the boundaries.

These are traits that can be found in some of the greatest business and social innovators of our time. They are the Elon Musks, Steve Jobs and the Mahatma Gandhis who fit this paradigm of the Blue layer best. They are concerned only with the moment, they often act in a world only they can see, with less consideration for the reality around them, and with no inner division about realizing their vision.

How do we unlock the Blue layer then? How can we reactivate our kidful power?

We can begin by doing what children do to learn, experience and thrive. We can play. For every child, the entire world is a playground.

We can observe this playful approach in most nonhuman mammals. The young play amongst themselves to learn and practice the skills they will need growing up. Our method of learning intuition is playing.

Unfortunately, we quickly learn that work and play are two different things as soon as we go to school. The first is an unpleasant but useful and rewarding activity, the second an entertaining but unproductive one. What is even more fascinating is that the word "school" is derived from the Latin word *schola*, meaning leisure devoted to learning. This is the original meaning of school, and it is how it was for centuries before the industrial revolution forced us to focus mainly on efficiency and productivity.

For most of us, playing is confined to mindless practices to distract and entertain the mind. Children, however, are fully invested in playing. For them, playing is the reality and they are fully engaged with it.

According to Professor Csikszentmihalyi's work, to create the state of *flow*, we need to invest ourselves in autotelic[17] experiences. Experiences that we do for the sake of the action itself rather than for ulterior motives. Exactly what we do when we play. When we do that, we learn to become more than what we were, and from there we can unleash the full potential of our intuition.

We must be aware however of not bringing our productive mindset in our practice of playing. Productivity is all about creating an outcome. When we play with the result in mind, however, it is no more an autotelic experience. We keep measuring our actions against the expected result, and the whole process quickly becomes a task or a chore, riddled with tension and disappointment.

The sages too recognize that playing is the ultimate spiritual practice, the one that gets us closer to that happiness, joy and bliss we described in the Violet layer.

Playing is also a practice of subtraction. When we enter a playground, different rules apply. We can let go of the beliefs and conditionings we hold as truth in our working environments, we liberate our mind from the noise of our thoughts, we create the space for ideas to emerge.

When individuals unlock the potential of the Blue layer, they become

---

[17] The term "autotelic" derives from two Greek words, auto meaning self, and telos meaning goal. It refers to a self-contained activity, one that is done not with the expectation of some future benefit, but simply because the doing itself is the reward.

aware that life is not simply about keeping our body and soul together, but that there is a greater purpose. Those who embrace this way of thinking have a drive to fully live that greater purpose. They constantly seek ways to reach a deeper meaning in what they do, to fully express their God-given gifts, and ultimately to make a positive difference. These individuals are the transformers of the world, not the chasers of the next paycheck, fame or job.

When the culture of an institution embraces the potential of the Blue layer, the institution becomes home to honest and authentic conversations. It understands and fulfills the needs of its people, offering them greater meaning and higher purpose in their endeavours. It grants empowerment and ownership to all stakeholders and creates a natural sense of collaboration. Such institutions have a higher tolerance for risk-taking, and understand the worth of learning from mistakes.

Institutions capable of accessing the Blue layer are inherently intuitive, they constantly look out for serendipities, and are always open to embrace spontaneous bursts of insights and illuminations. Only thereafter do they harness the logic mind to make innovation real.

Boundless innovators - whether individuals, institutions or movements - adopt the sequence of first harnessing the intuitive mind, and then using the power of reason to take ideas to the next level of manifestation. This formative power of reason is encapsulated in the layer of grosser awareness laid out in the following chapter.

# 2.6 *Manomaya Kosha* - The Yellow Layer



> *Logic pervades the world; the limits of the world are*
> *also the limits of logic.*
> Ludwig Wittgenstein

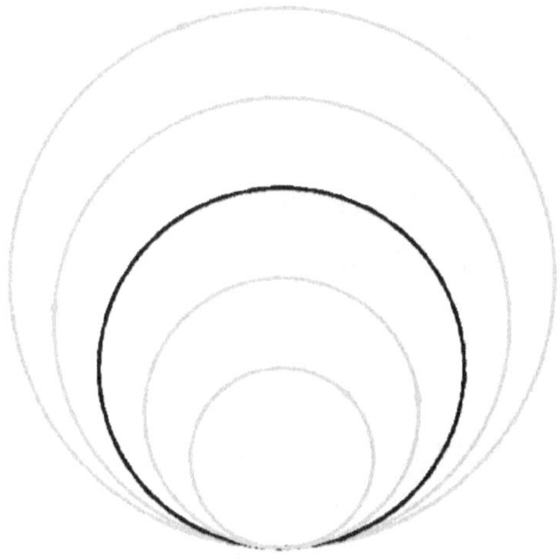

Billy Beane, the baseball general manager whose story was the subject of Michael Lewis' bestselling book, *Moneyball: The Art of Winning an Unfair Game,* and who was portrayed by Brad Pitt in the 2011 film adaptation, is no stranger to the power of *Cognitive Intelligence.*

Faced with one of the most mundane and minimal budgets for player salaries of any team in the US Major League Baseball in 2002, Beane, manager of the baseball team, the Oakland Athletics at the time, managed to throw a cognitive curveball into the mix; steering his team away from their dire straits and directly on the path of baseball fame with a new, analytical and evidence-based approach to the game.

Competing with the likes of the Boston Red Sox and Chicago Cubs for talent, Beane realised that something had to change in order for the team to make an impact in the league. With an annual budget of $44 million for new talent (compared for example to the New York Yankees' $125 million in payroll that season), the club found itself fighting for the tadpoles of the talent pool.

Not satisfied with the team's limited situation, Beane reached out to Harvard alumnus Paul DePodesta, who along with having a degree in economics, also had a talent for baseball statistics.

Hired as Beane's assistant, DePodesta - along with Beane - mined decades of data on hundreds of individual players in order to figure out the best strategy for recruiting better players. The strategy, based on the advanced statistical model developed by baseball writer Bill James, honed in on what traditional scouting means often overlooked: attributes — what to many — would seem abstract and irrelevant.

Bill James himself began his journey into baseball writing following a stint in the United States Army. Most of Jame's initial writings emerged during his night shifts as a security guard at the Stokely-Van Camp's pork and beans cannery following his return from Korea.

Whilst most writers at the time focused on the grandness of the game, James offered a different analysis, posing left field insights gleaned from interviews with players and offering alternative analysis centred on questions such as "which pitchers and catchers allow runners to steal the most bases". The following piece would then present data and analysis in order to offer an answer. This strange take on the game was niche enough to publish, catapulting James to legendary status amongst baseball aficionados over the following decades.

This rudimentary form of empirical analysis in baseball would later become known as sabermetrics. The term originates from the acronym SABR, which stands for the *Society for American Baseball Research* (founded in 1971) and was coined by James himself. Sabermetrics followed in the spirit of James' writing and gave accurate insights through objective analysis of past evidence.

Beane and DePodesta adopted this atypical way of analysing the game. They realised that the players overlooked by the most common statistics of that time were often undervalued on the bidding market. Together, they began searching for bargain baseball players, those who flew under the radar but would score runs according to the data.

Despite pushback from baseball scouts, Beane's analytical approach made baseball history. The Oakland Athletics became the first team in over 100 years of American League baseball to win 20 consecutive games.

Soon after, in the season's wake, teams such as the New York Mets, New York Yankees, San Diego Padres, St. Louis Cardinals, Boston Red Sox, Washington Nationals, Arizona Diamondbacks, Cleveland Indians, and the Toronto Blue Jays, all hired full-time sabermetric analysts.

***

Such is the power of the Yellow Layer - originally known as *Manomaya Kosha* - the sheath that, in the *Pancha Koshas*, contains the faculty of reason. The word *Mana* refers to the cognitive mind through which we make sense of the world via the agency of the five senses.

It is at this layer of awareness that we first experience objectivity of our subjective existence. In our journey of growth as a toddler we access this layer once we begin to associate forms and shapes. We become capable of imagining things and adding colours, features and other attributes to our insights.

*Imagination* - the product of the Yellow layer that corresponds to innovation - helps us with the first step of moving anything from the ethereal world into the mundane world. What we channel in the Blue layer is an illumination or a notion, something that cannot yet be described, that which is still relatively unreal. To make it real, or relatively real, we use imagination, a product of the Yellow layer.

Mystics recognize imagination as the sight you use to see the things that you cannot see with your eyes. This faculty helps us *reason* with things that we have only *felt* to be true before. The Yellow layer is the layer of reasoning, of calculative logic where we release our thinking mind's mighty power. The more the faculties of this layer are developed, the more we can make sense out of what we have intuitively felt all along. Sense-making allows for the mind to express further creativity and discover new ways forward for every perceived problem or situation.

Using our Cognitive Intelligence - the faculty of the Yellow layer - we can see the connections between things, we can recognise patterns and build models that help us make sense of what is happening within and around us. Using data and knowledge, we are able to have a new and deeper perspective on reality, beyond our own subjective experience of it. This is exactly what Billy Beane managed in the field of sports, as many other brilliant minds do across all domains of human engagement.

Cognitive Intelligence allows us to consciously choose our response to events and situations. Anytime we activate the faculties of this layer we are able to step above the clouds and turbulences of emotions and reach a space where the air is clearer, and we can integrate different perspectives about the challenges ahead of us.

At the Violet layer, through Spiritual Intelligence, we experience a connection that is so pure and holistic that we cannot discern the object from the subject of the experience. Then, through the Intuitive Intelligence of the Blue layer, we become aware of the separation, we recognise the experience as something other than ourselves. Still, the experience or intuition has no form or shape so we cannot truly comprehend it. Because we cannot put attributes on it we are unable to manifest it into actions or to share it with others.

Cognitive Intelligence gives form and shape to what our intuition has conceived so it can begin to manifest in the world. When in this layer, our imagination helps us place characteristics and attributes to entities, and we recognise ourselves as separate from others and from the world. This is where we develop our sense of self.

It is at this layer that we begin to perceive or, as many philosophers and scientists argue, create space and time. The nature of space and time is indeed a compelling subject that has captured the interest of many brilliant minds over the centuries. Immanuel Kant, in his *Critique of Pure Reason*, wrote that 'Space is not an empirical concept which has been derived from outer experiences. For in order that certain sensations be referred to something outside me (that is, to something in another region of space from that in which I find myself), and similarly in order that I may be able to represent them as outside and alongside one another, and accordingly as not only different but as in different places, the representation of space must already underlie them."

Kant argues that space is a feature that our mind uses to read and understand the physical world. More than two centuries later, neuroscience seemingly confirmed what Kant had anticipated. In 2014, Edward and May-Britt Moser were awarded the Nobel Prize in Physiology or Medicine, for their discovery of the grid cells; a type of neurons within the entorhinal cortex whose firing patterns resemble a hexagonal grid. These neurons activate when we navigate an open area, allowing us to create a cognitive map of the space around us and understand our position in it.

Similar studies have been conducted on the relationship of our mind with time. Talking about the death of a friend, Albert Einstein said that "people like us, who believe in physics, know that the distinction between past, present and future is only a stubbornly persistent illusion." For him, time was not absolute, only that which is relative to the observer.

In their effort to understand how the brain processes space and time, the team led by Edward and May-Britt Moser discovered that our brain does not have an internal clock ticking, at least not one like your wristwatch, measuring time in hours and minutes. Instead we have multiple biological clocks using experiences and memories to track time. Each one of these biological clocks, uses different time scales and different signals and triggers to do its work. In short, our brain creates a subjective perception of time by organizing into a sequence of discrete memories our continuous flow of experiences.

Without getting into a debate whether space and time are created by the mind or just experienced by it, what is clear is that both spatial and time information are subjective. They are fundamental in any innovation endeavor as they create the subjective frame for imagination to work, inform how we interpret reality, and how we see ourselves in relation to everyone and everything else in the world, and how we give substance to our ideas and intuitions.

A key role in the sense-making work of our Cognitive Intelligence is played by language. Language is a uniquely human capacity. Some animals may learn to associate words to an abstract concept or object, but only humans can combine words to make meaningful sentences.

We use language as a medium for exchanging information and for creating and managing social relations. Philosophers, linguists and scientists have explored and debated the relationship between language and the human ability to think for centuries. According to Benjamin Whorf[18], language shapes our thoughts and emotions and informs how we perceive

---

18 Benjamin Whorf, American linguist and fire prevention engineer, 1897 - 1941

reality. For John Stuart Mill[19], language is the light of the mind, and for Ludwig Wittgenstein[20], the boundaries of one's world are defined by the limits of their language. Peter Carruthers argues that "natural language is a necessary condition for human beings to be capable of entertaining at least some kinds of thought". Even with the various different and competing perspectives, it is clear that language plays a fundamental role in our ability to think and process reality.

Professor Angela D. Friederici, director at the Max Planck Institute for Human Cognitive and Brain Sciences in Leipzig, and her team discovered a fibre tract in the brain called *Fasciculus Arcuatus*[21]. It is like an informational backbone through which data is transported between the various parts of the brain that process language.

A fascinating aspect of this fibre tract is that it only exists in adult humans, not in toddlers. Which means that whilst our language capability is native, it only fully develops through our growth. Another crucial discovery is that a person's native language creates only negligible effects on the Fasciculus Arcuatus variations. That seems to confirm the Universal Grammar theory defined by Noam Chomsky[22], according to which a universal system for grammar is innate to human beings.

Space, time and language therefore are deeply interwoven with our cognitive potential, so it is no wonder that humanity has always given so much relevance to our thinking abilities compared to the other abilities.

---

[19] John Stuart Mill, English philosopher and political economist, 1806 - 1873

[20] Ludwig Josef Johann Wittgenstein, Austrian-British philosopher, 1889 - 1951

[21] Fasciculus arcuatus is latin for curved bundle and it is a bundle of axons that connects the Broca's area and the Wernicke's area within the brain.

[22] Noam Chomsky, American linguist, philosopher, cognitive scientist, historian, social critic, and political activist

Scientists have tried to measure (cognitive) intelligence since the 19th century. Alfred Binet[23] and Theodore Simon[24] developed the first (cognitive) intelligence test in 1904, and it was focused on logical reasoning, rhyming words and the ability to name objects. The term "IQ", used to refer to the measure of intelligence was coined a few years later, in 1912, by the psychologist William Stern. Since then it has been improved upon, and even if its validity as a measure of intelligence is disputed by many, it is still considered an effective way to measure human intelligence and is used in many different contexts.

IQ, however, leaves out an essential part of our cognitive faculties; curiosity. As professor Francesca Gino affirms in her article in HBR aptly titled *The Business Case for Curiosity*, "Most of the breakthrough discoveries and remarkable inventions throughout history, from flints for starting a fire to self-driving cars, have something in common: They are the result of curiosity."

Einstein, a typical example of cognitive brilliance, said about himself, "I have no special talents. I am only passionately curious."

More recently, Pulitzer prize-winning American journalist Thomas Friedman even coined the term Curiosity Quotient to emphasize its importance. Curiosity is a vital component of Cognitive Intelligence, one that allows us to grow and expand our faculties, avoiding the risk of getting stuck within the boundaries of what we know. Curiosity is the spark for imagination, logic and knowledge are its fuel.

Despite this truth, most organizations' configurations reward only attention and concentration, essential for efficiency and productivity. They believe that value-creation lies in answers and solutions, convinced that anyone can ask questions while only a few can provide answers. Yet, as

---

[23] Alfred Binet, French psychologist, 1857-1911
[24] Theodore Simon, French psychologist, 1873-1961

Krista Tippett wrote in her book, *Becoming Wise: An Inquiry Into the Art of Living*; "Questions elicit answers in their likeness. Answers mirror the questions they rise, or fall, to meet."

So, the truth is that if we want different answers, we must first learn to ask new questions. If we aim for groundbreaking innovations, we must not shy away from asking curious and courageous questions, the ones for which we have no answers yet.

Again, to access the faculties of the Yellow layer, we are called to embrace a practice of subtraction, using curiosity and the power of questions to explore what we do not understand. As Frank Herbert said, "the beginning of knowledge is the discovery of something we do not understand."

The Yellow layer is the layer from which most individuals and organizations are operating and have been operating for most of the last decades. Since the advent of the first industrial revolution, science and technology have created quantum leaps for humanity. The speed with which the world has been accelerating, thanks to technological innovation and scientific research, is mind-boggling. Most of the things we consider normal nowadays were material for science-fiction novels only two decades ago. These innovations are thanks to our well-expressed Yellow layer of awareness.

However, we should be careful to avoid the risk of thinking that the only things worth exploring are the ones we can comprehend and process with our cognitive mind. Imagining is not innovating. There are other faculties integral to the innovation process, as we have seen in the previous two chapters, and will see in the next chapter. This has become amply clear in the last 25 years.

"Ideas are plentiful, innovations are few," the age old adage of the Silicon Valley goes. This is partly so because it takes a cradle of many energies to carefully infuse life into an idea.

When we either get stuck in the Yellow layer of Awareness through "paralysis by analysis", or falsely believe that the 'might of the mind' will take our idea into innovation, we always fall short in our innovation goals. We need to breathe life into that which we have developed through logic. Infusion of life, the function of the Orange layer of awareness, laid out in the following chapter, will help you with it.

# 2.7 *Pranamaya Kosha* - The Orange Layer



*We are like islands in the sea, separate on the surface*
*but connected in the deep.*
William James

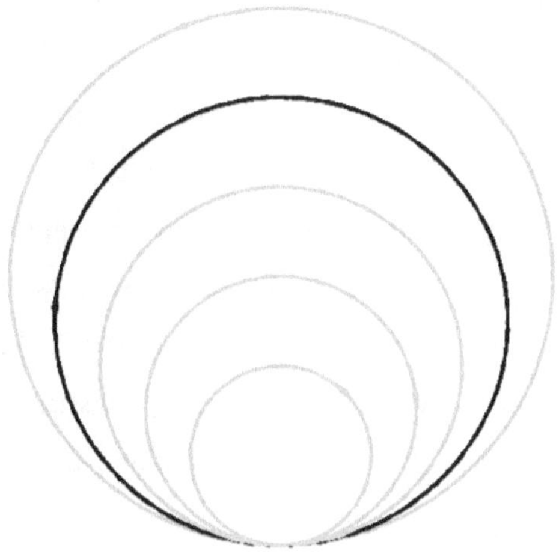

In the year 1948, a year after India's independence, after acquiring a degree in metallurgy and nuclear science from Michigan State University, a young Dr. Verghese Kurien returned to his homeland. Forsaking a lucrative US job, Dr. Kurien joined a run-down government research creamery at a meagre salary of 275 rupees a month as a way to repay the government for sponsoring his education abroad. He had earlier approached his uncle, Sir John Matthews, the first finance minister of independent India, to get his governmental bond cancelled. But to his dismay, the request was spurned. So, Dr. Kurien was left with no option but to serve the creamery.

Predictably, in Anand – the village where he was employed - Dr. Kurien often found himself fretting. To begin with, the then conservative village was wary of accepting him, a stranger. As he recalled, "I could not get a house because I was a Christian, a bachelor and a meat-eater. I lived in a factory garage which had an improvised bathroom and no proper ventilation."

Considering that he possessed a degree in Chemical Engineering and Nuclear Science, Dr. Kurien's discomfort with the dairy job was not a matter of surprise. He carried out his job reluctantly, and on weekends he would travel to Bombay (now Mumbai) on the pretext of work.

Despite this, Dr. Kurien found a saving grace in his boss, Tribhuvan Das. While Dr. Kurien tinkered with the primitive milk-processing equipment, he formed a close and endearing association with Das. Das, a Gandhian freedom fighter, had brought dairy farmers together after a strike in 1946 to form *The Kaira District Co-operative Milk Producers' Union* (KDCMPU), that would collectively purchase their milk. Das' philosophical ideas on social reform would prove to have a lasting impression on Dr. Kurien's mind, and it would be he who would later convince Dr. Kurien to stay in his dairy job.

In 1948, India was a free country. But her villages still desperately sought freedom from hunger and grinding poverty. Arid Anand was no different, the land, unfavourable for agriculture, was home to hundreds of impecunious cattle-owing smallholder farmers who were routinely exploited by private dairies and larger milk suppliers. KDCMPU was working to change things for the better for them.

Dr. Kurien was drawn towards Das' movement. Irrevocably. The farmers' pathos had stirred in him a resolve to reform. He felt a profound sense of empathy for the exploitation and penury experienced by the dairy farmers at the hands of the private traders. He knew that the very life-force of these farmers were inseparably interwoven with the bovines they cared for.

His connection to their plight awakened in him a social entrepreneur. Intelligently, he understood that the way to reform lay in uprooting the entrenched exploitative system and its replacement with a well-functioning milk cooperative that rewarded the farmers fairly.

There was another force that propelled Dr. Kurien's efforts to realize the mission of the cooperative. He felt a deep sense of understanding for the outrage and resignation Indian consumers felt when it came to buying their milk from the market. Milk from the private traders was so infamous for its adulteration that the British colonials in the past were known to say that "gutter water in London was biologically superior to the milk in India".

It was no surprise that Dr. Kurien quickly rose to the position of Executive Head of KDCMPU in 1950. No one understood the needs of the farmers better than he did. His strategies were well-crafted and fearlessly executed, at times it even meant locking horns with the political bosses of the day. While he was clear about his ability to make a difference, his confidence rested on his unflinching faith in the ingenuity, intelligence and abilities of the farmers.

Dr. Kurien's brilliant blending of the production of the masses and the power of technology benefited over 70 million rural households involved in milk production. "Innovation cannot be mandated or forced on people. It is everywhere, a function of the quality of the people and the environment. We need to have enough skilled people working in a self-actuating environment to produce innovation," Dr. Kurien once said.

Based on strong democratic foundations, Dr. Kurien's cooperative became a leading example of a thriving, transparent organization. The operational efficiency, process designing, execution strategies and resource allocation stemmed from ideas of equity. Blurring the economic boundaries, he opened the membership (at Rs 10) to all who wished to shoulder the weight of responsibility. Furthermore, the decision-making power was entrusted in the hands of the farmers; with each member having a single vote regardless of who they were. To further farmer's empowerment, Dr. Kurien placed policy-making in their hands, while entrusting the task of policy implementation and execution to the specialized professionals.

For many Indians, Dr. Kurien's name is synonymous with 'Operation Flood'. Operation Flood went on to monumentally transform India from a milk-importing nation to the largest milk producer in the world. Most remarkably, Operation Flood benefitted more than 10 million dairy producers in 81,000 cooperatives. Nationwide, it poured five million tons of milk annually - to over 1,000 cities, feeding milk to nearly 250 million people.

Operation Flood also had a significant sociological impact. It assigned a pivotal role to the farmers as the owners of their cooperatives. The operation was also praised as a boon to the rural women - milch cattle in India are mainly tended by women - in at least two ways. Firstly, through the milk movement many got empowered financially. Secondly, they were enlightened by ideas of science and modernity learned from their visits to the processing and cattle-feed plants.

Dr. Kurien's leadership was both agile and dynamic, but most importantly, it was buttressed by complete trust and support of the dairy farmers. Dr. Kurien never drank milk, in fact he was not fond of it at all! Yet, such was his empathy for the dairy cause and his constituents, the farmers, that his personal preference did not matter to him.

Dr. Kurien's story is a brilliant and inspiring odyssey of a social innovation that transformed rural India for the better over five decades. His extraordinary achievement was driven by his unique ability to place himself in the shoes of dairy farmers who relied on the traders to meet their daily needs, coupled with an energetic understanding of the insecurities felt by his fellow humans going about fulfilling their subsistence needs.

Part II: Awareness Informs Configuration

***

Dr. Kurien's story is an example of what it means to successfully operate from the Orange layer of awareness, the layer in which we are beginning to bring life to that which we have made sense of in the *Manomaya Kosha,* the Yellow layer. At this grosser layer of awareness we take manifestation to the next level. We infuse energy into the ideas and imaginations built in the Yellow layer.

This layer is called the *Pranamaya Kosha,* and it marks our existence because not only are we present in the physical plane, but we are also in a relationship with it.

In this layer of Awareness, our inner world - whether as a child or as an adult - starts expressing outwardly in the physical plane. Our sensations and emotions start to crystallize into visible configurations. Things start becoming "real", thoughts turn into words, and ideas into blueprints. Our dreams and vision get *infused* with *Prana.*

The word *Prana* roughly translates to 'life-force' from Sanskrit, and it refers to the vital energy that moves through each one of us. It is considered to flow in currents, in and around the body. The energy meridians that permeate through any living being is *Prana.* Breath is also *Prana* expressed in its subtlest material form. Emotions that flow through us is yet another manifestation of *Prana.* It is this life-force, or *Prana,* that is the secret ingredient that makes things real in a unique kind of way.

Have you ever wondered why children today are so natural with technology and gadgets?

Today's children feel an unconscious 'nativeness' with technology, a nativeness that comes from their energetic (*pranic*) alignment with technology.

Perhaps you have a grandmother who makes a special sauce that others are not able to replicate. She seems to have a knack for that dish. That mysterious energetic (*pranic*) relationship she has with that dish creates the alchemy of the dish.

It is this unconscious 'nativeness' that one feels when doing something that makes him or her feel that he or she is ordained for it.

The above are examples of how the Orange layer of awareness contributes to innovation.

The idea of energetic alignment is not a faraway concept to us. Innovation-driven organizations understand this at an intuitional level. Google has famously designed its Mountain View campus to stimulate creativity among its employees. Leaders give careful attention to creating chemistry between scientists who research together. These are ways to harness the Orange layer of awareness and create energetic alignment between entities in order to boost innovation.

The greatest innovators and achievers go beyond the boundaries of their thinking mind to create that alchemy of the Orange layer with their work or mission that others do not. We can all create that alchemy - that *pranic* connection - through sheer application. Dr. Kurien is a testimony to this.

The faculty of the Orange layer, the *Pranamaya Kosha*, that infuses life into our imagination is Social Intelligence, a term that is a fair abstraction of this faculty. For Social Intelligence, we relate closely to the definition offered by Sean Foleno; "Social Intelligence is a person's competence to optimally understand one's environment and react appropriately for socially successful conduct."

For the purpose of this text, we have overlooked some of the more recent definitions of Social Intelligence. Instead, we have approached it through the lens of consciousness, acknowledging what the mystics consider as Social Intelligence. It is considered to include emotional literacy (well-represented by the vast body of recent work labelled as Emotional Intelligence) and Ecosystemic Awareness (to be elaborated further).

Let us examine both components of Social Intelligence in further detail.

The concept of Emotional Intelligence is quite recent. It was coined by researchers Peter Salovey and John Mayer only in 1990. Salovey and Mayer defined Emotional Intelligence (EI) as "a type of social intelligence that involves the ability to monitor one's own and others' emotions, to discriminate among them, and to use the information to guide one's thinking and actions."

The word "emotion" comes from the Latin word *emovere*, meaning to "move out, remove, agitate". The Orange layer bestows upon us the ability to experience and process the energy of emotions - which is one manifestation of *Prana* - moving in and through our body. The more we master this capability, the more we can make emotions work for us, instead of against us, particularly when it comes to social environments. After all, for human beings - but also animals are not much different in this sense - the regulation of social behaviour is essential to our wellbeing and, pertaining to the subject of this book, also to innovation. This is what Dr. Kurien effectively did with the dairy farmers of post-independence India.

Our ability to deal with our own and others' emotions is a critical factor for functioning successfully in the world. No surprises then that the exploration of the emotional and social aspects of human nature have attracted thinkers across history, cultures and disciplines including art, spirituality, philosophy, psychology and neuroscience. All trying to unveil how emotions are triggered and, more importantly, if and how we can channel them to our advantage.

Being able to harness Emotional Intelligence and channel the energy of our emotions is essential to infuse our ideas with life and thus transform them into action, a step without which not even the best idea, intuition or imagination can fully manifest into an innovation.

The second - perhaps more crucial - component of Social Intelligence is Ecosystemic Awareness (EA), an awareness that helps us see our environment as a whole of which we are a part of.

This whole is a living organism composed of living beings, is governed by the laws of nature, and has an inherent geometry. It has its own life force and has got its own rhythm with which its different stakeholders connect to each other.

Ecosystemic Awareness is being aware of the energy of the space that we are part of. We notice the idiosyncrasies, motives, self-interests, needs and perceptions of the stakeholders within our ecosystem; all of which originate either from the *conditioned reflexes* or the *primordial nature* of the stakeholders within our ecosystems.

Our *conditioned reflexes* include our coping mechanisms, our need to belong, our primitive self-interest to survive, and all other motives arising out of our life experiences. Many of us have grown up with the belief that if we do not have people around us, we will be lonely and miserable, or worse, possibly soon perish. Or, if we are alone, we will be unhappy. When we are aware that such conditioning exists within our ecosystem, we are able to respond more effectively. EA helps us do that.

After generations and generations of poverty under colonial rule, the desperation to survive was what mattered most to the farmers of the cooperative to which Dr. Kurien belonged. He also well-understood the hopelessness of the farmers from generations of failures and the subjugation under bureaucratic authoritarianism in post-colonial India.

The awareness of our *primordial nature* starts with the simple recognition that we are awareness having a human experience. Humans have an innate yearning towards things they love doing; the things that realize their human potential.

Given a choice between work that will help them express their gifts, talents and strength, and work that is mindless and mundane, our inclination is to go with the former. If you would give people the choice between work that resolves our divisions and unifies humanity, or work that debilitates or exacerbates divisions in humanity, they would choose the former. Ecosystemic Awareness is being aware of this *primordial nature* of awareness.

The farmers of Dr. Kurien's cooperative felt an inherent fellowship with the bovines under their care, a love that comes from being part of a civilization that revered cows from the onset of time.

Dr. Kurien had a knack of understanding the dynamics of his ecosystem unlike anyone else. Using his Ecosystemic Awareness, Dr. Kurien could surf the waves of the natural forces of the ecosystem that he was part of and create one of the greatest socioeconomic innovations of our times. This despite being an outsider who was, in his own words, "a Christian, a bachelor and a meat-eater".

*Prana* therefore goes beyond the individual self and what happens within us. It also exists within your wider ecosystem. It moves between people, and flows within spaces.

Like with waves at sea, our individual life-force (*Prana*) can be reinforced or be cancelled by the ones around us. Sometimes we feel completely at home with someone we just met. We feel a sense of natural chemistry with that person, we experience resonance of ideas, and before we know our conversation takes us to a moment of spontaneous ignition of inspiration. This is Social Intelligence in action, unleashing unforeseen potential through the union of two or more life-forces finding their counterparts in each other. Ground-breaking innovations result from such catalysis.

After all, humans are a social species and, despite our love for the myth of the hero slaying the dragon on his own, nobody can really achieve anything significant alone. Behind every hero there is a social field without which there would be no hero at all. As Greg Satell perfectly states in his book, *Mapping Innovation: A Playbook for Navigating a Disruptive Age,* "any significant innovation involves an incredible diversity of problems that need to be solved, from theoretical and engineering challenges to manufacturing and distribution hurdles. There is no silver bullet, and no one person—nor even a single organization—can provide all the answers alone."

In 1998, sociologist Randall Collins published a book called, *The Sociology of Philosophies: A Global Theory of Intellectual Change*, the result of 25 years of research to understand how thinkers and ideas connected through history and across continents. After mapping over 3,000 philosophers and mathematicians from many parts of the world and historical periods, he found out that creative thinkers tend to cluster. It may be to collaborate or to compete, whatever be the case, they motivate and inspire each other. Thus, the achievement of one cannot be isolated from its cluster. Just think back to the golden age of physics, between 1840 and 1930. In this cluster, there were eminent minds such as Einstein, Planck, Tesla, Marconi, Westinghouse, Madame Curie, the Wright Brothers, Emmy Noether, Edison and others; the achievement of each one of them must consider the influence of all the others.

In fact, studies have shown that emotions are easily spread to others, more often than not unconsciously, via a phenomenon called emotional contagion. Various mechanisms have been proposed to explain this phenomenon, including mimicry, the action of the mirror neurons[25], and frequency resonance. Whatever the mechanism, the effect of energetic fusion between two configurations is real and we all experience it in our lives around us daily.

We often notice this happen with players who switch teams in sports.

---

[25] Mirror neurons are a class of neuron that modulate their activity both when an individual executes a specific motor act and when they observe the same or similar act performed by another individual."

A player who seemed mediocre before moving often experiences a huge burst in performance in their new setting. He feels right at home with the *Prana* of the new club. The energy of the fellow line-mates, the coaching style, the culture, the system of execution - all collectively known as systemic life-force - feels fully synchronous with the life-force of the player, resulting in the leap in his or her performance.

The faculties of the Orange layer allow us to sense, channel and influence the energy around us; an ability that is fundamental if we wish to transform ideas and imagination from their ethereal form into gross energy and make an impact in the world.

*Prana* flows not only within and between people, but also between spaces. Many studies have explored the role of environments and places on people's ability to be creative and innovate. From the science of consciousness we know that space has its own energy signature that interacts with the energy of the people in them.

As others' energy may reinforce or cancel ours, the energy of a place can do the same to us. That explains the pervasive adoption of ancient science of space and spatial harmony like *Vastu Shastra*[26] and *Feng Shui*[27]. These sciences give us algorithms to align spatial energy, enhance healthy vibrations and neutralize the unhealthy ones.

By nurturing the faculties of the Orange Layer we become aware of the intangible but crucial energetic dimension of our innovation process, including the interrelationship between the energy of our ecosystem and the people who operate within it. Being Innovators are masterful in harnessing life-force and infusing power into everything they have conceived

---

[26] Vastu Shastra is an ancient Indian science of harmony and prosperous living by eliminating negative and enhancing positive energies around us.

[27] The philosophy of feng shui is a practice of arranging the pieces in living spaces in order to create balance with the natural world. The goal is to harness energy forces and establish harmony between an individual and their environment.

through the faculties of the previous three layers of awareness.

If the Cognitive faculty of the Yellow layer gives us the ability to make sense of the world and imagine new paradigms, the Social and energetic faculty of the Orange layer helps transform our ideas into grosser energy forms. This ability to harness the *Prana,* the life-force, within and around us, is crucial to the creative potential of the boundless innovator.

If we are to create a tangible impact with our innovations, all this energy inside and around us must be harnessed to create something tangible. Like a combustion engine transforming energy into movement, the faculties of the next layer, the Red layer, helps us with the final step of materializing our innovations. The following chapter deals with that final transformation.

# *2.8 Annamaya Kosha* - The Red Layer



*Having a vision for what you want is not enough.*

*Vision without execution is hallucination.*

Thomas A. Edison

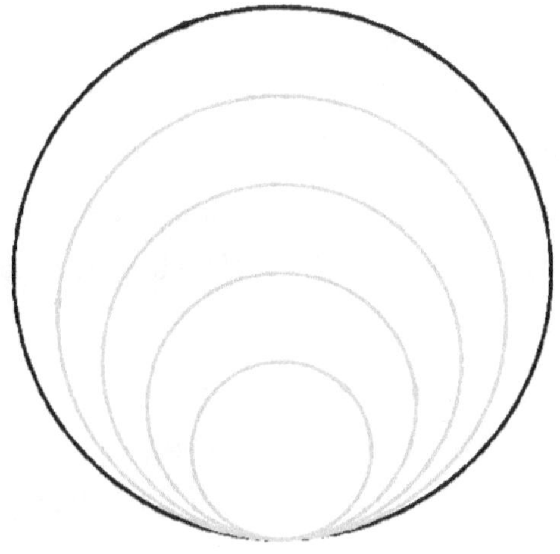

James Dyson is a name synonymous with the vacuum cleaner. The British inventor, seen in recent years as one of the few captains of industry to back Brexit — Britain's departure from the European Union — did not become a billionaire for want of trying.

Dyson's love affair with the vacuum began back in 1979. Whilst the rest of the world found itself captured by the sounds of Pink Floyd's *The Wall* and The Clash's *London Calling*, this particular Brit found himself dismayed with what was going on in the world of household utilities.

In an interview with Inc magazine, Dyson told his interviewer that he was disappointed with what was on offer: "I'd purchased what claimed to be the most powerful vacuum cleaner. But it was essentially useless. Rather than sucking up the dirt, it pushed it around the room. "Taking inspiration from a local sawmill Dyson imagined that the same technology could be shrunk down and built into a vacuum cleaner, negating any need for a bag and ensuring the device would not lose suction and become less useful over time: "I'd seen an industrial sawmill, which uses something called a cyclonic separator to remove dust from the air. I thought the same principle of separation might work on a vacuum cleaner. I rigged up a quick prototype, and it did."

His eureka moment was just that, a moment. What followed were 15 years of highs and lows, and consisted of thousands of prototypes to get what would finally be the cyclonic vacuum that first cracked the market. "By 2,627, my wife and I were really counting our pennies" Dyson wrote in Wired in 2011, "by 3,727, my wife was giving art lessons for some extra cash."

Finally after a staggering 5127 attempts, Dyson's now famous vacuum was a reality. "It didn't happen overnight, but after years of testing, tweaking, fist-banging, and after more than 5,000 prototypes, it was there."

But it did not stop there, Dyson's innovation would still have to be licensed to a company, and - once again - this was a long and burdensome process. Changing the vacuum zeitgeist would not happen overnight, and the young innovator would spend three years travelling the world and trying to convince old-school vacuum companies that they should join him in the vacuum revolution.

When Dyson approached Hoover in 1981, the deal was particularly rotten. A clause agreement about any meeting was included that anything that came out of the discussion would belong to Hoover. After asking them to remove the offending clause, Hoover refused. Dyson recalls in his autobiography *Against All Odds* that he wouldn't cross paths with the company again until 1995 — by which time the inventor would have overtaken them in the marketplace. According to Dyson's autobiography, in that year, Hoover's VP of Europe admitted on the *Money Programme* that the company "regretted not buying my invention, because they would have seen to it that it never saw the light of day".

The reason was as simple as it was cynical: "These vacuum makers had built a razor-and-blade business model reliant on the profits from bags and filters. No one would license my idea," Dyson explained in his *New York Magazine* article. 'Not because it was a bad one, but because it was bad for business."

In *Against All Odds,* Dyson records his bewilderment at this. "It really was extraordinary, and quite unexpected. Every single one of them seemed to miss the point: that here was an innovation of real benefit to the consumer, a massive leap from a crappy old carpet sucker to a cleaner of total efficiency and undiminishable power".

With the vacuuming world only interested in the sale of bags, Dyson continued to journey around Europe looking for a home for his innovation. "I survived on a sort of mañana attitude: tomorrow would always be better. You have to think like that, otherwise you just can't go on." Eventually, Dyson turned West and managed to license his product to an American company, but even this he would later call a "disaster".

Following his various failed escapades in drawing others into his vacuum revolution and after years trying to avoid having to manufacture the product himself, Dyson would eventually decide to manufacture his innovation alone. Broke after the various failed deals, he would find himself putting his own house on the line to do so. But this was really just the beginning.

As Dyson wrote himself in the Globe and Mail, over 5ooo failed attempts at creating an innovative product was "frustrating" at the same time, "it was also invigorating, exciting". This lack of urgency may come as a surprise, but ultimately it is this tension with not being satisfied with how the physical world is that is the driving force behind making any impact. Indeed, in the aforementioned Inc article, Dyson writes how he always sold "from the point of view of frustration, hoping that other people feel the same way".

So it is through hardship, frustration and continuous reiteration that innovation realises itself. Yet despite this the truth is we always think there is an easier way.

But, as Dyson himself notes "Not only do people cringe at the thought of failing, but we're also an impatient bunch. We want success fast; the quick buck, the overnight sensation, the teenage billionaire. And, for the highest return on investment." In reality this is often not the case.

***

When it comes to inventions and innovations, we are drawn to stories of spontaneous illumination, like the one with Newton and the apple. We like to believe that the idea that changed the world was thrust upon someone in an almost magical way. Similarly, when we become aware of an innovation or experience its impact, we might think it happened overnight.

However, the arc of fruitful innovations is often a long one, as the story of Dyson and many other celebrated innovators reveal. When it comes to innovations, it makes more sense to enjoy the ride than obsess over the destination. To manifest anything into the material world, we have to do diligent work.

Dyson's ability to see the positive side to the grind is the cornerstone of his success. For innovation rarely happens in a moment. For the fortunate few, this may not be the case, but for the majority, it takes diligent execution, complete detachment from outcomes, and patience to turn an idea into reality.

In his article, Dyson writes of a litany of failures that never saw the light of day. But a museum of failures is still more useful to humanity than a mind full of successes never realized. Indeed, as the adage goes, it is better to fail and do something than to fail and do nothing.

This relentless execution is an important impetus behind the Red layer of awareness, originally known as *Annamaya Kosha*. The Red layer represents the grossest awareness of all the layers. *Anna* in Sanskrit means matter, and *annam* literally means food. The Red layer of awareness is the one of materialization, one where awareness solidifies into matter, nourished by energy (laid out in the previous chapter) and food[28].

To create an impact in the world, even the most excellent and inspired ideas must transform into something concrete. Be it a physical product or a virtual service, it must acquire a form that others can experience. This is what is meant by *materialization*, the step of manifestation that corresponds with the Red layer.

If you recollect, when we access the Violet layer's Spiritual Intelligence, an *intention* is bestowed upon us. That Intention becomes a shapeless *illumination* when we tap into the Blue layer's power of Intuitive Intelligence. Then, through the strength of *imagination* of the Yellow layer's Cognitive Intelligence, it moulds into an idea. The Orange layer of awareness is where our ideas and imagination get *infused* with life, thanks to Social Intelligence.

Still, nothing has yet fully manifested in the world.

The Red layer is where our innovation idea acquires its gross form. Once done, others can experience our innovation with any of their five senses.

The faculty of intelligence that corresponds to *Annamaya Kosha* – the Red layer - is Physical Intelligence. Physical Intelligence informs our

---

[28] Here we mean food in the most broader sense, from the food we eat to the resources an organization needs to operate.

capacity to *materialize* things.

On the physical plane, Physical Intelligence is responsible for transforming energy or matter from a subtle or gross form into another gross form. Sand is turned into silica, silica into glass, and glass into bottles.

Everyday innovators do such materialization in little ways. They break, blend and bend things to create new things. They apply their resourcefulness and turn the fire department into emergency first responders. Or they make single-use plastic out of petroleum, which later they develop into construction raw material. This is the intelligence we observe in many craftsmen, artists, engineers and developers. They use their imagination and thinking to develop new things. These innovations happen in the physical plane; in the realm of time and space.

Holistically, however, materialization means more than just transforming matter from one form to another. It is also about harnessing the potential of the four intelligences discussed in the previous chapters, and manifesting from the Unmanifest; the space where no matter or form exists, but the properties and potentiality of all matter and form exists. Visionary entrepreneurs are renowned for their ability to gather all the other intelligences and channel their potential into something concrete. This function of materialization is rounded off in the following chapter.

In her 2014 TEDx talk called *You are the Art,* Laüra Hollick, an Award-winning Artist and Visionary Guide, says that art is about making our imagination real, bridging the inner world with the outer one. She explains that there are two steps in any artistic process. The first one is to imagine our new reality; it could be a new world or a new self. The second step is to go for it. To press ahead until the imagined becomes real, until, using her words, "you make your imagination so real that it is undeniable."

This is the role and the power of Physical Intelligence; to make the reality we have conceived through our Spiritual, Intuitive, Cognitive and Social Intelligence so real that it becomes undeniable. Like Dyson did through his relentless experimentation.

In a broad sense, Physical Intelligence is the capacity for diligent execution needed to manifest anything into the world. It takes a special breed of innovators to apply Physical Intelligence and materialize things.

From Gandhi, Martin Luther King or Dyson, we know that that capacity is an essential part of any innovation endeavour. When we think about the 37 years it took Mandela to go from prison to the end of his presidency to finally manifest his innovation of the 'Rainbow Nation'[29], we cannot marvel at greater perfection, for that was what was meant to be.

For such innovators, time is not measured in minutes or hours, or not even years or lifetimes, it is measured in the quantum of the impact their innovations made on humanity and the planet. Sometimes it takes the whole of a lifetime, sometimes it is many lifetimes in the making. But when accomplished, it immortalizes them. As Nietzsche once wrote, "with regard to everything that is perfect we are accustomed to omit the question as to how perfection has been acquired, and we only rejoice in the present as if it had sprung out of the ground by magic."

Yet, when it comes to hiring people for innovation roles, Physical Intelligence is often overlooked. Organizations look for creative talents, brilliant thinkers, and emotionally aware people. The capacity for diligent execution is often considered a secondary requirement, or sometimes even overlooked. However, without this intelligence, no ideas can manifest into impactful innovations.

When Angela Duckworth, the author of the bestseller *Grit: The Power of Passion and Perseverance*, was teaching math to seventh graders, she soon realized that IQ was not a good predictor of which students will succeed and which one would struggle. What really made the difference

---

[29] Rainbow Nation is a term coined by Archbishop Desmond Tutu to describe post-apartheid South Africa, after South Africa's first fully democratic election in 1994.

was grit as the ability to hold steadfast to a goal through time. After that, she researched grit's effect on people's performance, discovering how grit is a critical factor for long-term success in nearly every realm of life.

There seems to be a natural bias in society towards talent as the main factor to achieve remarkable results. And talent is obviously essential, however by shining the spotlight on it, we risk overlooking everything else. The underlying message we convey is that other factors, like grit, do not matter as much. However, as Duckworth's states, "talent counts but effort counts twice." Effort is the needed catalyzer to transform talent into results.

To manifest anything meaningful in the world, we are then called to master Physical Intelligence. As Dyson's story perfectly illustrates, his relentless experimentation and diligent execution led him to create the impact he envisioned fifteen years before. However, achieving the desired goal is not the most important thing, as Henry David Thoreau said, "what you get by achieving your goals is not as important as what you become by achieving your goals."

Individuals who have nourished the faculties of the Red layer show high levels of endurance and resilience. They infuse presence and intensity in their actions, yet no sense of urgency. These individuals radiate the *Zen*[30] aura that comes from mastering their craft. They find fulfilment in and through practice and discipline without being attached to the outcome.

When institutions imbue the power of the Red layer in their culture, they exhibit excellence in everything they do. Industrious and hardwork-

---

[30] In this context, with Zen, we refer to a feeling of peace, oneness, and enlightenment that allow an individual to stay present and non-judgmental. The monk and teacher Shunryu Suzuki says that Zen is not some kind of excitement, but concentration on our usual everyday routine."

ing, they are characterized by steady growth. They keep relentlessly improving not only what they do but also how they operate.

To unleash and nurture the faculties of the Red layer, we must invest in cultivating a prototyping mindset. A mindset that recognizes that we pursue but never reach a stage of perfection. When we embrace reality's impermanence and experience everything as a prototype, our work becomes a source of attainment. This attitude of openness is typical of novices — that in Zen Buddhism is called Shoshin — the beginner's mind; an attitude essential for those who want to keep improving on their neverending journey to mastery.

# 2.9 The Wholistic Nature of the Being Innovator



You should be convinced by now that the class of Being Innovators we have examined in the last five chapters are a different breed. They focus on the *self* over processes and outcomes as a means to unleash boundless innovations.

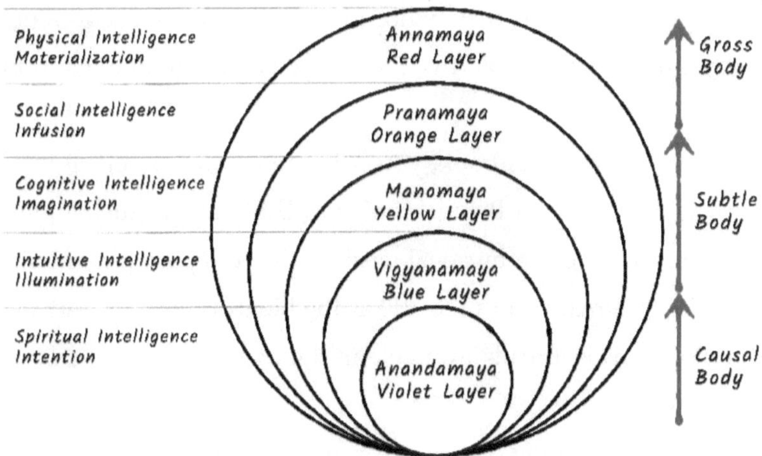



While everyday innovators recognize that materialization begins and ends in the physical plane, the Being Innovators recognize that the origin of materialization is in the metaphysical plane. With them, all five intelligences uniquely fuse into a higher form of *wholistic intelligence*[31] that is capable of manifesting things out of the Unmanifest.

They can intention from their causal awareness, move it through their subtle awareness and onto the gross plane, thus making something out of nothing. A sculptor might intention the creation of a vase and manifest it in its final form. The intention for the vase comes to the sculptor from his causal state of awareness, begins finding energetic form in his imagination while he is in the subtle states, and finally materializes into a vase in his gross states of awareness. This is the arc transformational innovations take to become real.

This is not a faraway concept for any of us. The most inspired painting artists apply their wholistic intelligence to paint. They Intention what wants to express through their brush, hold that Imagination in their awareness, and then create the painting. Musicians like Santana follow this route to create their music, same with renowned craftsmen who shape their vision to enter the world, or great entrepreneurs who realize their ideas into solutions. They all rely on their wholistic intelligence that combines in unique ways the faculties of all five layers and spawns boundless innovations.

In the next part of this book, you will join us on a practical journey that makes any innovator a Being Innovator. Undertaking such a journey involves understanding the mystical wisdom that the pure potentiality of any innovation is already out there. That the blueprint of any and all unrealised innovations is already available in the *causal library*, even that of past and future ones.

The idea that no living being is ever extinct might seem like a radical

---

[31] A symbiosis of all the five intelligences that is greater than the sum of its parts.

thought. To say that even the revival of a dinosaur is conceivable may seem like insanity to the rational mind.[32] Yet how many innovations we consider normal today were deemed to be crazy fantasies only a few decades ago?

Once we understand the omnipotent nature of the *causal library*, we also realize our own power to innovate boundlessly.

Thence the question, "how do we access that library and innovate from there?"

It is only through a process of subtracting the layers of our conditioning, and expanding our awareness, that we can access that library. As we expand our awareness, we access the subtle and causal realms of the *self*, thus opening a channel to the causal library. In this experience of *non-duality*, we greatly shorten the distance between intention and manifestation.

All of creation happens when intention and manifestation come together. Imagine you wish to create a birthday video. You start with the intention of the product. Thereafter, through the application of some or all of the subtle and gross intelligences, you manifest the video. In some cases, the creation takes a few minutes, in other cases, much longer.

The distance between intention and manifestation is informed by how expanded our awareness is. The more wholistic our awareness is, the shorter the distance between intention and manifestation. So much so that when we as innovators can fully realize our wholistic awareness, intention and manifestation can be instantaneous. This is what the mystics refer to as miracles.

---

[32] As we write this manuscript, humanity is in a lockdown due to the COVID-19 pandemic. Among the gloom and doom of this time, we have been presented with the news that a bird that has been reported long-extinct has been spotted recently in Africa. The Aldabra white-throated rail bird was declared extinct, a victim of rising sea levels almost 100,000 years ago. However, it has recently been spotted – leaving scientists perplexed as to how the species has come back to life.

# SUBTRACTION

We are all capable of miracles. Some highly creative people can create something from an idea in a minute. Mythology is full of such stories. We call such innovators magicians, alchemists, or wizards.

In the gross world though, there is a vast distance between intention and manifestation. It can take a long time for an innovation to come to life, and sometimes never. Our conditioning is what widens that distance.

The limited human mind is conditioned to operate within the dimensions of space and time, making manifestation an intense and laborious process. This comes with its own unique set of challenges.

We are conditioned to believe that there are certain things we are able to do, and certain things we are not. Or certain things are possible in life, while certain others are impossible. Or that it can take years for dreams to come true. Such beliefs widen the distance between intention and materialization.

To create breakthrough innovations, we must first break free of the boundaries of our limited mind. The more we can expand the mind and access the subtler realms of awareness, the more boundless the innovations become.

In 1895, Lord Kelvin confidently stated that "heavier-than-air flying machines are impossible". Eight years later, the Wright brothers completed their first flight. Space travel was thought to be the stuff of science-fiction until the early 20th century. Then, two rocket researchers, one in the USA and one in the USSR, almost simultaneously found a way to reach the velocity needed to escape gravity. A trip to Mars is today considered absolutely feasible. It is not that we are smarter today than those before, it is just that every new innovation pushes the boundaries of what we deem possible a little farther.

Being Innovators the likes of Tesla, Einstein, Ramanujan[33], and Da Vinci knew this secret; that of boundless innovation. They unleashed their wholistic intelligence to generate innovations that seemed superhuman to others, thus making them legends.

Being Innovators are alchemists who engage all the faculties of the five layers of Awareness — the Spiritual, Intuitive, Cognitive, Social and Physical Intelligence — to create their own reality. This gift is what makes innovators, Being Innovators. They know that their potential is boundless. Through pure application, they are capable of manifesting any innovation. All it takes is to expand their awareness to integrate all the layers and fully leverage their corresponding intelligence.

In the next part, we will lay down the journey that you can undertake to unleash the boundless potential of the Being Innovator that is innate in you.

---

[33] Srinivasa Aiyangar Ramanujan (1887 -1920) is a famous Indian mathematician who was largely self-taught. His story is told in the 2015 movie *The Man Who Knew Infinity.*

# Integration Moment

The journey into awareness is an inward one, it is a journey of subtraction. The existing maps typically work by adding to what we already know, but additional knowledge does not help us expand our awareness. That is why we need a different map. We found ours going back more than three thousands years, in the wisdom of the *Vedic* sages of India; the *Pancha Koshas*, or the five sheaths. From that simple, holistic and timeless map we derived our five layers model for spawning boundless innovations.

| Layer of Awareness | Kosha | Corresponding Intelligence | Action |
|---|---|---|---|
| VIOLET | Anandamaya | Spiritual Intelligence | Intention |
| BLUE | Vigyanamaya | Intuitive Intelligence | Illumination |
| YELLOW | Manomaya | Cognitive Intelligence | Imagination |
| ORANGE | Pranamaya | Social Intelligence | Infusion |
| RED | Annamaya | Physical Intelligence | Materialization |

The following table gives you a summary of the five layers of Awareness and their corresponding innovation levers.

Each layer unlocks the faculties of one of the five main human intelligences. We are really continuously flowing and floating between all the layers, however, in our wakeful state, we mostly operate from the Red layer, with some level of expression of the Orange and Yellow layers. It is only when we can access and integrate all layers through a process of subtraction that we can fully become the Being Innovator and unleash innovation breakthroughs.

## Self-enquiries:

- *Looking at the five intelligences, which one do you feel is the most important for an innovator? What makes it so important?*
- *Which intelligence do you think is more developed in your organization or environment? What would be the benefits of developing the others?*
- *What is the opportunity, if any, for introspection for you or your working environment?*
- *Have you ever experienced one of those "a-ha!" moments when the solution of a challenge becomes self-evident before your eyes? When did it happen? Are you able to deliberately create those moments?*

# Part III:

Awareness Fuels Innovation

*A hero ventures forth from the world of common day*

*into a region of supernatural wonder: fabulous forces*

*are there encountered and a decisive victory is won:*

*The hero comes back from this mysterious adventure*

*with the power to bestow boons on his fellow man.*

Joseph Campbell

When Mohandas Karamchand Gandhi set sail to South Africa to be the lawyer for a Muslim merchant in 1893, he could not have dreamt of the impact he would one day make upon the world.

Aged just 23, Gandhi had already spent several years studying in London - absorbing different lifestyles, religions and cultures - in pursuit of practicing law as his father, a successful lawyer and governmental official, had done before him.

What had brought him and his family to South Africa was not success, but failure. Upon returning to India from London, he found he lacked the knowledge of Indian law and was also not the most outspoken when it came to trials. His practice collapsed soon after.

Consigned to defeat, he took up work in colonial South Africa for a period of 12 months and for a fee of £105.00, serving as legal counsel to a merchant named Dada Adbulla.

The case in question was a lawsuit between the Porbandar brand of Dada Abdulla's firm against a local Transvaal merchant. Local traders were not experienced in English, and needed somebody with both a solid grasp of the language and of the law to assuage their problems.

Soon after his arrival in South Africa, Gandhi was asked to travel to

Pretoria for work, a journey that he travelled in first class on a train. Onboard, a white passenger asked that Gandhi be removed from the train, seeing as at the time it was illegal for a "coolie" - as Indians were derogatorily called - to be seated in first class.

The white railway officials were quick to comply, and despite showing them his ticket, Gandhi was pushed out of the train and into the cold night.

With indignation, an infuriated Gandhi sat on a bench in the railway station in Pietermaritzburg. He would later write in his autobiography that "the cold was extremely bitter. My overcoat was in my luggage, but I did not dare to ask for it lest I should be insulted again, so I sat and shivered".

It was here, insulted, cold, and alone, that he had an awakening. His job was not to become a successful lawyer or a successful tradesman. It was to make a difference. He began to think about his "duty" in the world.

As Gandhi listened to the call to adventure, he realized that the hardship he suffered was only a superficial symptom of the deep disease of colour prejudice. So, it would be cowardly for him to go back to India; instead, he decided that he would "root out the disease and suffer hardships in the process". The next day, he decided to continue his journey to Pretoria unabashed. His journey to being a Mahātmā, meaning a great soul, had begun.

Getting chucked off the train for being non-white was not happenstance, but part of general life in South Africa. As such, the next stage of Gandhi's journey was marred by the same prejudice as the previous day, but this time in an even more insulting manner.

The journey from Charlestown to Johannesburg was to be made via stagecoach. In those days, it was considered improper for whites to be sat with non-whites. Hence the white man in charge of the stagecoach refused Gandhi passage inside. "Your ticket is cancelled," the man told Gandhi, directing him instead to sit outside with the person driving the coach.

During the journey, the leader of the coach who had sat Gandhi outside in the cold demanded he move once more to allow him space to smoke. As Gandhi writes in his diary, "he took a piece of dirty sack-cloth from the driver, spread it on the footboard" and told him to sit at his feet.

Gandhi protested, explaining that this was one insult too many. Upon this, he began to be beaten severely by the man, who tried with all his strength to remove him from the coach. "The passengers were witnessing the scene, the man swearing at me, dragging and belabouring me, and I, remaining, still," writes Gandhi. "He was strong and I was weak".

The passengers, aghast at this pitiful sight, cried out for the beatings to stop. Embarrassed at the distress he was causing his passengers, the white man in charge of the coach halted his hurtling fists, told the other servant to move aside and sat down in the newly vacated outdoor seat.

Gandhi, however, remained seated. Devastated, spirit broken, disillusioned with life, he arrived in the town of Standerton in Johannesburg. On that day, he had crossed a certain threshold, committed never to return to his old life of subservience.

In Pretoria, Gandhi began to expand his mind. On his first day, he ran into one of the directors of the South Africa General Mission, a Christian man named Mr. Baker. After Gandhi conceded that he knew little of his own religion, Hinduism, and even less of the other religions, Mr. Baker, delighted at Gandhi's openness, asked him to join him in daily prayer. He also provided Gandhi with many religious books to read.

That night, Gandhi went to bed, wondering how he would ever understand another religion without understanding his own. He could not, he concluded, and so decided there and then that "I should not think of embracing another religion before I had fully understood my own."

Off the back of his apprenticeship under Mr Baker, Gandhi crafted his worldview and understood his own philosophies better. Such philosophies drew on from several cultural and personal wells of inspiration.

About his talks with Mr. Baker and the Christians, Gandhi writes that the idea that "renunciation was the highest form of religion appealed to him greatly". Of Mohammed, he found his "bravery and austere living" commendable. But, as he writes, he had long "crossed the Sahara of atheism" and saw value in all theologies, not viewing one as better than the other. During his time in Transvaal, it is thought that the 24-year-old Gandhi had 80 books on religion on his shelves.

Then came the various examples of passive resistance from across the world: the Chinese boycott of American goods, the Russian revolution of 1905, Chief Bambata's actions against the hut tax that led to the Zulu rebellion, and the ongoing Irish strategy of non-cooperation. All of these world events he referred to several times in his articles in *Indian Opinion,* a magazine he encouraged Indians in South Africa to launch in order to mobilise their peaceful resistance. They all lent to his apprenticeship for what was yet to come.

It was in Pretoria where Gandhi made the first public speech of his life. It occurred at a meeting where Gandhi wanted to paint a picture to the Indians living there of their dismal condition.

He spoke of the concept of truthfulness in business and how, for Indian emigrants especially, this was tantamount in importance. "The conduct of a few Indians was the measure of that of the millions of their fellow-countrymen", and to those in South Africa, the petty squabbles between the " Hindus, Musalmans, Parsis, Christians, Gujaratis, Madrasis, Punjabis, Sindhis, Kachchhis, Suratis and so on" were nonsensical.  The meeting, Gandhi concluded, was well received, and he began teaching many who had attended it. In his early attempts at public activism, he was shaping his vision for the future.

His time in Pretoria, Gandhi writes, gave him space to "make a deep study of the social, economic and political condition of the Indians". At the time, he had no idea that this would prove invaluable in the future, but

Gandhi would later describe his early years in South Africa as "a most valuable experience of my life". It was here where he started to crystallize his vision and become a living force.

"While I was working with the Corps[34], two ideas which had long been floating in my mind became firmly fixed. First, an aspirant after a life exclusively devoted to service must lead a life of celibacy. Secondly, he must accept poverty as a constant companion through life. He may not take up any occupation which would prevent him or make him shrink from undertaking the lowliest of duties or largest risks."

Paramount were the ideas of the British art critic John Ruskin, in which Gandhi found much truth. In his autobiography, Gandhi details the first time he read Ruskin's *Unto This Last,* in which he "discovered some of my deepest convictions" were reflected.

The teachings, he writes, were "that the good of the individual is contained in the good of all", "that a lawyer's work has the same value as the barber's, inasmuch as all have the same right of earning their livelihood from their work", and "that a life of labour, i.e., the life of the tiller of the soil and the handicraftsman, is the life worth living." It was the last point that informed Gandhi's quest the most.

Then came Leo Tolstoy, whose *The Kingdom of God Is Within You* "overwhelmed" Gandhi for its "independent thinking, profound morality" and "truthfulness". The book teaches that man's highest duty is to love his fellow man and resist all violence, a philosophy that was to inform Gandhi's future activism.

The *Bhagavad Gita* - one of the most important texts in Hinduism,

---

34 The Natal Indian Ambulance Corps was a group of stretcher bearers created by Mahatma Gandhi for use by the British during the Second Boer War. It consisted of 300 free Indians and 800 indentured labourers. Gandhi was bestowed with the Kaiser-i-Hind and other medals by the British for his work in the Boer war. It was given up by Gandhi after the Jallianwala Bagh massacre in 1919.

with tenets and ideas stretching back thousands of years - Gandhi writes, "deepened my impression, and Tolstoy's *The Kingdom of God Within You* gave it permanent form".

In Gandhi's own words, the New Testament "really awakened me to the rightness and value of Passive Resistance". The ideas proclaimed in the Sermon of the Mount confirmed his opinions about what was right, cementing them where he "least expected it."

At the culmination of his years-long quest, Gandhi had a revelation; the idea of nonviolent resistance against the colonial forces. When the idea dawned upon him, he fully knew it was his mission forward. This he later came to call *Satyagraha,* meaning insistence on the Truth. He defined the two main principles of *Satyagraha* as insistence on the Truth and dependence on the force inherent in Truth.

As a man of pious means, he felt a deep knowing that this was the right path at every level. "The means may be likened to a seed, the end to a tree; and there is just the same inviolable connection between the means and the end as there is between the seed and the tree," Gandhi writes in his journal, *Hind Swaraj*[35] .

The great idea behind *Satyagraha*, Gandhi says, is to change the mind of the wrong-doer, not to force him. Winning means getting along with the enemy to make what is wrong right again.

*Satyagraha* is not the same as passive resistance. In fact, Gandhi stresses that a distinction is of the utmost importance in explaining what it means to conduct *Satyagraha*, which he often describes as "soul force" in his works.

The main difference is that many movements described as passive - such as the suffragette movement - also involved a lot of physical action

---

[35] Literally translates to Indian Home Rule

(beatings, firebombings etc.). But, as Gandhi writes, "brute force had absolutely no place in the Indian movement in any circumstances", and the *Satyagrahis* (those who practiced *Satyagraha*) never used physical force.

This is because, generally speaking, those who live by the sword die by the sword and would have fewer occasions for offering *Satyagraha* in the first place.

Another distinction lies in that *Satyagraha* can be offered to those nearest and dearest, whilst passive resistance by definition suggests an element of hatred for the other party. In this sense, as Gandhi himself writes, the story of Jesus Christ is not one of passive resistance but of *Satyagraha*.

For a world used to fighting fire with fire, the idea of *Satyagraha* was a radical innovation, one that went counter to all logic.

Although Gandhi's innovation of *Satyagraha* was birthed by many parents, it was the key to Gandhi's successes, in both South Africa and later in India. This innovation of righteous means of persuasion, a lesson learned from many places, was central to how Gandhi operated after he was first removed from the train due to his skin colour.

It would not be until 1906 - more than a decade after his arrival in South Africa - that Gandhi would have his theory of passive resistance vindicated. In that year, the British administration in Transvaal passed the Asiatic Law Amendment Ordinance (Black Act) to control the entry of Indians into the colony. This meant that every person of India or Chinese heritage who entered the region would have to register themselves. If they did not, they would have to leave. If they did, they would have to keep hold of the document at all times lest they be fined or thrown in prison.

Gandhi himself writes of that text: "I shuddered as I read the sections of the Ordinance one after another. I saw nothing in it except hatred of Indians... Better die than submit to such a law. But how were we to die? What should we dare and do so that there would be nothing before us except a choice of victory or death? An impenetrable wall was before me, as it were and I could not see my way through it."

When Gandhi arrived at Transvaal, he took no time setting up a campaign to end the mistreatment of the Asiatic population in the province. Together with the Chinese community, Gandhi asked the Indian and Chinese population to vow never to submit to the Black Act, no matter what the government threatened. "Merely disobeying the government's laws will not be enough." Gandhi declared, "You must have no hatred in your hearts. And you must cast away all fear."

This vow became known as the *Satyagraha Oath*. It marked the very beginning of the eight-year-long *Satyagraha* campaign in South Africa and the birth of the larger *Satyagraha* movement.

*Satyagraha* turned out to be the boon for both Gandhi and humanity. This principle came to Gandhi before he had words to describe it (the name itself came from a nominal prize Gandhi offered in the *Indian Opinion*).

On the closing day of registration, only 511 out of 13,000 Indians had signed up to the Black Act. Still, the government rejected the pleas of the population. In peaceful retaliation, more than 2000 registration certificates were burnt, with vivid images broadcast to the world of the ensuing bonfire.

It took many years of broken promises and guarantees until the Black Act would be repealed. By then Gandhi had galvanised the downtrodden communities of the region, and the tactic of *Satyagraha* had left an impact on those who had taken the vow.

An important part of Gandhi's time in South Africa was dedicated to the creation of the Tolstoy Farm, a clear homage to the author who inspired his innovation. Gandhi describes the farm as having "nearly one thousand fruit-bearing trees and a small house at the foot of a hill with accommodation for half-a-dozen persons". In the farm many *Satyagrahis* resided, working and living off of the land.

Part III: Awareness Fuels Innovation

Gandhi states that "the weak became strong on Tolstoy Farm and labour proved to be a tonic for all", there where hard work and a simple life contrasted that with the outside world. That said, this would not be the real setting for Gandhi's innovation. Instead, the deep thinker would look back to his homeland, India, which still faced many of the same problems he had witnessed in South Africa but had yet to feel the impact of *Satyagraha*. This was thanks to repeated requests from both his friend and mentor Gopal Krishna Gokhale, a senior leader of the Indian National Congress[36] who played a central role in the independence movement in both South Africa and India.

Gandhi would write that "if Gokhale had not played this stellar role, the South African problem would never have resolved". Gokhale, who funded much of Gandhi's escapades in South Africa, was instrumental in getting Gandhi back to India permanently, telling him repeatedly from 1901 onward to return, and explaining how he had been out of the country for too long to understand how to bring change about in India.

"Every word of Gokhale glowed with his tender feeling, truthfulness and patriotism. Gokhale prepared me for India". Eventually, on February 27, 1914, Gandhi would write to Gokhale that, "I propose to leave for India in April. I am entirely in your hands. I want to learn at your feet and gain the necessary experience. My present ambition is to be by your side as your nurse and attendant. I want to have the real discipline of obeying someone whom I love and look up to. I propose to use the funds you have sent for our passages". Ten months later, Gandhi would embark for his home. His innovation would find a new playground where it would go on and write history.

Gandhi brought *Satyagraha* to India in 1915 and was soon elected to the Indian National Congress party. He began to push for independence

---

[36] The principal nationalist movement of pre-independence India

from colonial rule, always insisting that the freedom struggle be based on his innovation, *Satyagraha*.

He organized resistance to a 1919 law that gave British authorities carte blanche to imprison suspected revolutionaries without trial. He started by organizing nationwide civil disobedience to British rule. He would exhort the masses to march in resistance, be subject to brute force by the colonial army and be thrown in jail en masse, however never to respond violently.

An exasperated Britain responded brutally to the resistance, mowing down hundreds of unarmed protesters in the Amritsar Massacre. There, acting Brigadier-General Reginald Dyer ordered troops of the British Indian Army to fire their rifles into a crowd of unarmed Indian civilians in Jallianwala Bagh, Amritsar, Punjab, killing at least 379 people and injuring over 1200 other people.

An innovation that could solicit such a brutal response from a rattled colonial force established in the minds of the revolting Indians that, for the first time, the freedom struggle was working. The Jallianwala Bagh tragedy only increased India's determination to pursue harder with *Satyagraha*. Historians would say that this was the moment that the freedom struggle became real in India. By then, the entire nation of India was enamoured by the idea of peaceful resistance, and further force from the colonial authorities only fortified the wide use of *Satyagraha* as the real weapon of war for the Indians.

Following the tragedy, Gandhi pushed even harder for home rule, this time encouraging boycotts of British goods and organizing mass civil disobedience. One of the most significant moments of this journey centred on the Salt Tax of 1882, which prohibited the native Indian population from selling salt, an obvious staple required for cooking.

Gandhi took to several acts of civil disobedience in order to repeal the tax. He encouraged local Indians to take salt water from the sea and farm salt themselves on their rooftops. He printed and sold his works en masse to spread the word of *Satyagraha.* Most famously, he kicked off a 21-day march from his spiritual retreat near Ahmedabad, India, to the Arabian Sea coast, a staggering 240 miles.

The journey on foot, famously known as the Salt March, took place between March and April 1930 and culminated with Gandhi evaporating salt by the sea.

Gandhi continued his journey southward along the coast. Five days into this stretch of the march, also known as the Dandi March, Gandhi was arrested. In response, a *Satyagraha* campaign was launched against the salt tax that gained widespread coverage across the globe.

Despite the coverage, no concessions were made by the British authorities. Instead, 60,000 Indians found themselves arrested for their role in the peaceful resistance.

The genius of the Dandi march lay in salt's ubiquity. Used by both the Hindu and Muslim populations of the subcontinent, it became a symbol of unity against a tyrannical rule. This, underpinned by the concept of *Satyagraha,* made the Dandi March the culmination of much of what Gandhi had learnt of the freedom struggle so far.

It would take another two decades before Gandhi would be rewarded for bringing *Satyagraha* into the world. His guiding star inspired years of protest, which showed that the Indian population would not subjugate themselves to violence in the face of unjust tyranny.

However, as World War II distorted the world stage and its priorities, the Indian population was asked to fight alongside their tormentors. Gandhi, and India, sided with the British, showing that, even after all this time, he had learnt not to hate his enemies but to conquer them with kindness.

Upon the end of the war, Gandhi, who had long ago given up being a lawyer after realising the oxymoronic nature of both practicing law and defying it, would use his innovation of *Satyagraha* to set the stage for one of the most impactful innovations of the 20th century, leading to the independence of his homeland India from Imperial British rule.

# 3.1 Becoming the Being Innovator



The Hero's Journey is a widely used model in story development. The model has been popularized by Joseph Campbell in 1949 in his book, *The Hero with a Thousand Faces*. Campbell called this basic narrative pattern the "monomyth". Later, in the late 80s it became known as the Hero's Journey.

The Hero's Journey carries great significance in the ancient traditions as it does in contemporary life and leadership.

In *The Rites of Passage* (1908), French ethnographer Arnold van Gennep observed a recurring pattern in indigenous societies. Every passage from one status or stage of life to another was marked by a ceremony or rite. It is fascinating that these rites have a similar structure based on three phases in all these different cultures.

In the indigenous traditions of Africa, India, Polynesia and the Americas, young men and women were - and still often are - taken through an initiation journey. A journey to help young adults attain mental and emotional adulthood to complement their physical maturation. Again, these initiation journeys typically include three stages: departure, passaging, and arrival.

The departure stage involves the shedding of the young adults' child self, which sees itself as an extension of its guardians or parents. This stage consists of cutting the emotional umbilical cord that keeps them dependent on the parent for their wellbeing, and experiencing separation (psychologically, physically, or both) from the guardians.

The passaging is the apprenticeship stage where – under the tutelage of an elder or teacher – the young adults are exposed to adulthood's many dimensions. They inquire and search for the meaning of life. This stage includes re-examining their life in relation to the opposite sex, community, and God.

Arrival is the stage where young adults embrace their authority as adults. They re-emerge as self-authored adults in full mastery of their faculties, and live life in full realization of their own infinite potential.

Campbell's journey similarly is divided into three acts and is divided further still into 17 stages, even if not all of them may be present in every hero's journey. In the following years, many thinkers have worked on the subject, sometimes creating variations of the structure.

The model has also moved outside the world of narrative and storytelling and it is now often adopted as a reference for personal development work. The Hero's Journey highlights the deep interconnection between the story's plot and character development. As the hero moves through the arc of the story, they undergo inner and outer transformations along the stages of their journey. Their transformation in turn shapes the story as it unfolds. The Hero's Journey is so successful because it accurately represents the process of transformation that each of us undergo as life-experiences force us to learn and evolve. It also offers an effective model to map the journey of any grand human endeavour.

For this reason, the Hero's Journey became the natural inspiration for our map of each person's journey of becoming the Being Innovator. As with the heroes and heroines of many stories we love, the journey of any innovation is as much one of ideas, choices, discoveries, gestures and facts, as it is a story of the personal transformation of the people involved in it. We are aware that a map is never the territory, however it is still probably the best way to explore it.

We created our Innovator's Journey map combining elements from the initiation journeys of indigenous traditions, the original work of Campbell, the 12 stages defined by Christopher Vogler in 2007, and the 9 stages identified by Phil Cousineau in his biography of Campbell published in 1990.

The Innovator's Journey is divided into three acts and nine steps (see image), and it is a journey that unfolds inside and outside us - as an individual, team or organisation. It might happen all at once, or it might take years like it did in Gandhi's life, or it might be a long sequence of iterations going back and forth through all three phases.

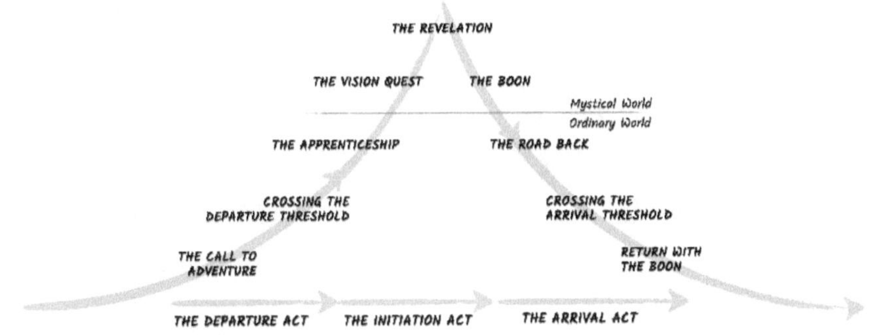


Gandhi's journey of innovating *Satyagraha* as a model for the freedom struggle of India is an apt example of the Innovator's Journey. The following section dives into the three acts of the Innovator's Journey.

# The Departure Act

This is when the innovator becomes aware of the challenge in the Ordinary World and decides to embrace the journey to change what exists and create something new.

## 1. The Call to Adventure: Hearing the Calling

The departure of an Innovator's Journey begins with an awakening. It may be triggered by an event like the **Pietermaritzburg** train incident in Gandhi's life, or it may originate from an inner awakening, a deliberate choice to change or evolve something. Whatever the source of the call, the innovator feels called to change something existing and create something new.

Yet, as we all know, becoming aware of something does not mean that we are going to act on that awareness. The choice to embrace the calling is influenced by many inner and outer factors, including fear, the level of self-confidence, available resources, external support, and so on. There could be many reasons to give up on a challenge before even beginning the journey. Only when the innovator has mastered those challenges and built enough motivation, within and around, does the journey begin.

## 2. Crossing the Departure Threshold: Committing to Change

The journey of any boundless innovation is one of transformation, a transformation that happens both within and around the innovator. This step is the moment when the innovator begins to create a personal connection with the worldly challenge. Whatever the problem of the world that the innovators are called to solve, it becomes personal to them. And that makes the whole journey way more difficult because it raises the stakes. Only the ones who are ready to challenge themselves, their knowledge, and their beliefs, can cross the threshold and set out on the Innovator's Journey.

This is the step when the journey becomes intentional. Here the innovator makes the deliberate choice to commit to the journey even if, most of the time, the destination is unknown. This was the choice of a beaten and broken Gandhi when he decided to remain seated on the stagecoach. In that moment he committed to something larger than himself, even if at that time he did not know the kind of journey he was stepping into.

# The Initiation Act

This is when the innovator ventures into uncharted territory within the Mystical World and is rewarded with the revelation of the new.

## 3. The Apprenticeship: Experimenting with Change

They say that when the student is ready, the teacher will appear[37]. Once the innovators commit to the journey, the world opens up to them. Thereafter, their objective is to learn as much as they can about the challenge they are facing. They research, find and acquire resources, sharpen their tools, and connect with whoever can help them in the journey. This apprenticeship attitude, or beginner's mind[38] draws the masters to the innovators. These masters that can take many forms; people, books, events,

---

[37] This widely used saying comes from an old Theosophical book titled Light on the Path, written in 1886 by Mabel Collins. The original statement is a bit more poetic, and it says; "for when the disciple is ready the master is ready also."

[38] Shoshin (初心) is a word from Zen Buddhism meaning "beginner's mind." It refers to having an attitude of openness, eagerness, and lack of preconceptions when

encounters, places, etc.

For Gandhi, the master took the form of Mr. Baker, the Christian who invited Gandhi to join him in daily prayer. But he also learned from the many books on religion, the past experiences like the Chinese boycott of American goods and the Russian revolution of 1905, and the work of John Ruskin and Leo Tolstoy.

In this step of apprenticeship, the innovators explore the challenge and become familiar with it. Most often, through research and experimentation, they are able to reframe the challenge in ways that open up the space for creative and previously invisible solutions to appear. They stretch themselves to the boundaries of what they know and can learn, and of what they can understand and connect with. In that moment, the voice of logic goes quiet and they begin to listen beyond. It is at this step that the innovators transition from the Ordinary World, the one they want to change, into the Mystical World where breakthrough ideas can be sourced.

## 4. The Vision Quest: Preparing for the New

Almost exhausted in his quest, the innovator sits before his work waiting for some inspiration to come through. A sense of impatience and confusion begin to cripple the innovator's conviction. He knows there is something out there wanting to be found, an idea that will change everything. Despite all the work and the learning, the way forward is still eluding him.

Richard Phillips Feynman, winner of the Nobel Prize in Physics in 1965 for his work on the development of quantum electrodynamics, said that most of the time he was in a state of confusion, an uncomfortable yet incredibly creative state where ideas emerge. Most of us approach innovation because we want results. Preferably predictable results. However, as

---

studying a subject, even when studying at an advanced level, just as a beginner would.

Feynman tells us, it is only when we become comfortable with living in a place of not knowing, that we can access breakthrough ideas. This is why insights often come when we are doing something else, as if our intuition needs some space to do its work. As Gandhi told, it was while he was working with the Corps that the vision of the innovative idea of Satyagraha became firmly fixed in his mind.

## 5. The Revelation: Receiving the New

The reward for the ones who muddle through confusion, chaos, uncertainty, failures, and the not-knowing, is the impending revelation. All of a sudden everything becomes clear in spontaneous epiphany, and the answer the innovator was looking for is there right before her eyes. This step is the tipping point of the Innovator's Journey when the destination becomes destiny.

What the innovator receives may not be the solution or the answer, it may not even be an idea yet. That might come later. The revelation is more of a whisper or the subtle sensation, elusive and real at the same time, that she is not only ready to find the solution, but also been invested to solve this challenge by the Universe. The one who reaches this point of the journey is infused with a burst of excitement, a surge of renewed energy. Everything looks possible from this new place.

It was only after a quest of a decade that Gandhi had his revelation, the idea of nonviolent resistance against the colonial forces. That revelation later became the well-known Satyagraha. The journey of innovation does not finish here, rather it has just begun...as Gandhi's story proves.

## 6. The Boon: Accepting the New

The first step after the revelation is one of opening the self and acceptance. The intuition needs a safe space where it can acquire form and shape. But it is also a challenging and scary moment in the journey of the innovator. At this stage, a breakthrough revelation might be still full of unknowns and uncertainties. The idea might feel crazy and too ambitious. It may ask the innovator to take a leap of faith without any safety net. When the innovator realises the impact that the idea could have on her world and herself, and how much she will have to risk bringing the Boon to the world, she might give up.

But the ones who accept the Boon are rewarded with a renewed sense of purpose, clarity and energy that will allow them to begin the final leg of their journey. This act is the one that will bring a breakthrough innovation into the world.

Gandhi told that when the idea dawned upon him, he fully knew it was his mission forward. Even so, it took many years for the idea of "peaceful resistance" to fully become *Satyagraha*.

# The Arrival Act

When the innovator embraces the new and begins the journey to bring the new into the Ordinary World to create an impact.

## 7. The Road Back: Experimenting with the New

The first step of the Arrival Act is one of experimentation and play with his idea. Here the innovator moulds substance around the intuition. To do so, he needs resources and support from the outside world. He creates prototypes, makes mistakes and learns. He must face the outer voices of rationality that try to water down the idea to make it more acceptable and predictable. Learning to navigate the Ordinary World is the key to this step. It is as much about learning to position himself against the opponents and naysayers as it is about using his power of reason and imagination to shape the innovation. With that thrust, the idea grows into a new product or service while the innovator acquires a new mastery.

To refine and shape his vision in the real world, Gandhi went through eight years of experimenting with Satyagraha to end the mistreatment of the Asiatic population in the province of Transvaal. Tolstoy Farm was the laboratory for prototyping his peaceful resistance and pious conduct. It was in this step, while sharing his experiments with others that the concept of Satyagraha became real and began creating a visible impact.

## 8. Crossing the Arrival Threshold: Unleashing the New

Alone and isolated in Alaska, a young American named Chris McCandless wrote in his diary that "happiness is only real when shared". The same applies to any innovation. It is only when shared that any innovation realises its transformational potential and creates an impact. This step is a pivotal moment in the journey of the innovator, a moment of choice. Something that the innovator has crafted, shaped, held and protected so it could grow into a fully formed innovation, is now ready to be released into the Ordinary World.

But releasing something implies a form of separation, accepting to let go of something so it can live a life of its own. It also means to expose what has been created to the final test of the world out there. What if the world will not understand? What if the world is not ready for such an innovation? Any failure of the innovation may be perceived as a personal failure of the innovator. Such a long and challenging journey would be for nothing. At this threshold, the innovator makes the deliberate choice to let go of her innovation and release it into the world so it can realize its full potential.

Despite the evidence of the incredible power of Satyagraha, it took

Gandhi more than ten years to decide to cross the arrival threshold and bring his vision to his homeland, India, where he found a brutal and aggressive colonization underway. Only an indomitable faith in his vision allowed him not only to push through the resistance he faced, but also to awaken a whole nation.

## 9. Return with the Boon: Final Mastery of the New

In this step, the innovation is finally out there. The threshold of fully releasing it has been crossed, but the journey is not over yet. Like a newly hatched seed, the innovation must be taken care of and protected so that it can bloom, and the world can harvest its fruits. Through the work of others, the impact of the innovation gets multiplied and becomes exponential. While the innovation begins a journey on its own, for the innovator is time to celebrate. Having undertaken the Innovator's Journey, he is now a Being Innovator. He looks ahead for the new journeys ahead.

The Dandi march was the key event that made the concept of *Satyagraha* universal, as it was able to unify both the Hindu and Muslim populations of the subcontinent against a tyrannical rule. Yet, it took more than two decades before the concept of *Satyagraha* manifested all its power, leading to the independence of India from imperial British rule. *Satyagraha* had to have many owners for it to realise its reason for existence.

# Integration Moment

Since time immemorial, the Hero's Journey is a widely used model in story development. It carries great significance in ancient traditions as it does in contemporary life and leadership. The Hero's Journey is so successful because it accurately represents the process of transformation that each of us undergoes as life-experiences force us to learn and evolve.

For this reason, the Hero's Journey became the natural inspiration for our map of each person's journey of becoming the Being Innovator. We created our Innovator's Journey map combining elements from the initiation journeys of indigenous traditions and various contemporary studies on life and leadership.

The Innovator's Journey is divided into three acts and nine steps, and it is a journey that unfolds inside and around us - as an individual, team or organisation.

The Departure Act is the stage when the innovator becomes aware of the challenge in the Ordinary World and decides to embrace the journey to change what exists and create something new.

The Initiation Act is the stage when the innovator ventures into uncharted territory within (the Mystical World) and he/she is rewarded with the revelation of the new.

The Arrival Act is the stage when the innovator embraces the new and begins the journey to bring the new into the Ordinary World to create an impact.

## Self-enquiries:

- *If you think about the important changes in your life - becoming an adult, marrying, changing work, moving to another country, promotions, having children - did you ever have a ceremony to mark the passage? How things would have changed if you had?*
- *Did you ever experience a rite of passage in your life? What impact did it have on you?*
- *Which of the steps of the Innovator's Journey do you feel is more challenging for you? What do you find more challenging?*
- *Thinking at the challenges you are facing right now, where do you see yourself or your team in the Innovator's Journey?*

# 3.2 How Awareness Fuels the Innovator's Journey

*Human beings are on a journey of aware-
ness, which has momentarily been inter-
rupted by extraneous forces.*
Carlos Castaneda

Anytime we face a challenge, or we need to solve a problem, or we want to change something existing, we have the choice to embrace the Innovator's Journey. The Innovator's Journey can be thrust upon us, sometimes even in painful ways - as it happened in Gandhi's life - or it can be a deliberate choice we make because we yearn to change something existing. In both cases, we must be ready to seize the moment and enter the journey.

However, let us make it clear; the journey is rarely linear and straightforward as represented in the image shown in the previous chapter. Almost always, it is messy and chaotic, with thrilling accelerations and abrupt stops, and with rewarding successes and painful fallbacks. Some steps may take an instant, while others may take years. Some journeys are quicker as we glide smoothly through some steps. Other journeys iterate back and forth through the same steps before moving forward. Further, as Gandhi's story teaches us, there can also be smaller journeys within the main journey.

As with all experiences in life, we can connect the dots of a journey only in hindsight, looking back at what happened. It would therefore be a mistake to read the Innovator's Journey as a linear process, a sequence of instructions to follow mechanically to create breakthrough innovations.

Instead, the journey is something that ensues when we expand our awareness. It is an inner journey before it becomes an outer one. Going from one step to the next is more about who we are, than about what we do. The map of the Innovator's Journey helps us less with going somewhere or achieving something, and helps us more with fully realising who we are, our potential to innovate. This map can help us sense where we are on our own journey, so we can make the best choices to prepare ourselves to move forward.

"How do I know where I am on my Innovator's Journey"? "What is the next step I can grow into in my journey of becoming a Being Innovator"? "How do I prepare myself for the next leap in innovations"?

The five layers of awareness that we have studied in part II are our guide to find the answers to such questions.

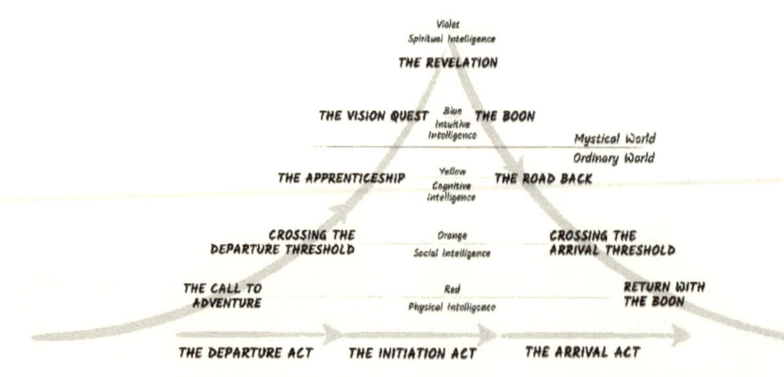


The Red, Orange and Yellow layers of awareness form the Ordinary World, while the Blue and Violet layers form the Mystical World. We are all constantly swinging between all these layers, often unconsciously. In every day, every moment, and every phase of our lives, we are fluctuating back and forth between the Ordinary and the Mystical Worlds.

These relentless movements and cycles are part of our human nature. However, in almost every area of our lives, our society favours linearity. Which is understandable. When it comes to productivity and performance, linearity has been a standard of the Western culture post the industrial revolution. Well-defined configurations with linear processes and journeys are favoured as they are easier to control, model and replicate to achieve efficiency. Even when it comes to creativity and innovation, we have become accustomed to the idea that the journey of innovation should be a linear one. So when the journey becomes messy, as it often does, we tend to think that there must be something wrong, something not working in ourselves or in what we are doing, individually and collectively.

Take a look at Gandhi's journey. Not a linear one, for sure. Some steps took years, others challenged him to go back before moving forward. There were failures and uncertainties almost at every step. It was, in short, a very human journey. A similar messiness can be observed with the journeys of other renowned innovators as well. Their journeys were more like rollercoasters, with extreme highs and deep lows. Yet, they did not evade it. Instead they embraced the journey and thrived in that struggle and messiness.

This nonlinearity played an essential role in their achievements, because the Innovator's Journey is one of great duality.

Someone with a managerial mindset is probably always operating within the Ordinary world; the Red, Orange, or Yellow layers. They have very little duality. No swinging in between grosser and subtler layers, no inner crisis or life-changing doubts. They seem very comfortable in their skin being where they are, with very little inner-division. Because they operate only within the Ordinary World, their innovations are typically incremental, not radical. That is because, when approaching innovations, people and organizations who operate in the Ordinary World favour predictable and manageable configurations, methodologies and processes.

On the other end of the spectrum, you come across many mystics and hermits, people who operate solely in the Mystical World; in the Blue and Violet layers. They also experience very little duality, they feel very comfortable within, having subtracted all their material thoughts and worries. They might have a set of dreams and inventions in their head, but they do not feel much urge to manifest them, and they do not experience any inner tension because of it. Again, they experience no duality within, but also deliver no innovation with real impact.

People who are going through all phases of the Innovator's Journey, however, feel strong duality within and around, because at some point they leave one world for the other. They move from the Ordinary World to the Mystical one, and sometimes back. Perhaps more than once. In that process, they have to find ways to connect with people operating within both worlds, being pulled both ways while trying to find their own balance.

Operating in duality can come with its costs. When the innovators leave the Ordinary World at the end of the Departure Act and step into the Mystical World, they might feel stretched by their inner duality. They begin questioning all their relationships, their work, the place where they live in, their values, their life standards. They start asking deeper questions about their true reason for existence, their purpose in life. They ponder, "do I continue as business as usual or do I try to reinvent a third way? "

All these inner divisions are symptomatic of the passage into the Initiation Act.

On our journey of becoming the Being Innovators, these inner tensions and emotions are clues that can help us understand where we are in our journey. If we are feeling inside rage, frustration, bitterness, resentment, anger, etc. with respect to our life, that is a sign that we are somewhere in the Departure Act. If we are feeling inner division, resignation, sometimes despair, hopelessness, surrendering in the not-knowing, momentary bursts of elation and then depression, then we are most likely in the Initiation Act. If we are feeling euphoria, elation, a sense of momentum, restless energy taking us forward, bliss, forgiveness, gratitude, infinite possibilities, etc., then we are most likely in the Arrival Act.

Once we become aware of where we are on the Innovator's Journey, we can prepare ourselves to open up for the next step.

The next step, however, will only ensue from our inner work. The journey requires for us to first access a subtler level of awareness. Only then will our inner resources be unlocked, and the following step appears as a natural evolution in the direction of becoming the Being Innovator. For this expansion of awareness to happen, a work of subtraction is needed.

Subtraction helps us peel away our conditioning accumulated over decades of upbringing and access the faculties needed to move forward. If those faculties are locked, we must remove the conditioning holding them back. Only then the journey will unfold naturally before us. There lies the power of Gandhi's journey. Not in what he had done but in who he became.

However, because the Innovator's Journey is not a linear process, what subtraction is being asked for at a given moment cannot be easily predicted. Hence, it is normal human tendency to try to bypass the inner journey in favour of arriving at the destination quickly.

Such a bypassing is not bad, per se. Those who seek to return to comfort quickly, or are not inclined towards self-discoveries and are content with incremental innovations, are better off with such a bypass.

But for those who are seeking to discover more dimensions of the self or harness breakthrough innovations, following the arc of the Innovator's Journey is a crucial exercise. This means embracing a journey of subtraction first; one that unlocks the layers of awareness one by one, paving the way for the nine steps of the Innovator's Journey.

This process of subtraction can either be transient or intransient. It is transient when we enter a *state* of subtle awareness - through meditation, mindfulness or other similar awareness-based practices - and we operate from that state for a short while during which time we may source solutions and answers.  The subtraction process is intransient when we enter a *stage* of subtle awareness - through the use of ongoing and structural practices to permanently unlearn and uncondition ourselves - where we remain permanently and innovate perpetually.

How far we get in the Innovator's Journey therefore depends on the state or stage of awareness from which we are creating. Let us walk together through the nine steps of the Innovator's Journey using the five layers of awareness as our compass.

# Influence of Physical Intelligence on the Call to Adventure

At the beginning of the Innovator's Journey, when we hear the inner or outer calling to change something existing, our amygdala — the older part of our brain, what we call the reptilian brain, one that responds to physical and ego threats — is triggered, and our survival instincts kick in.

"Am I in danger?" "Should I run from the threat or face it?" We ask ourselves.

At this step of the Innovator's Journey, our choices and actions are sourced from the Red layer. We are driven by our Physical Intelligence and the will to survive. It is a critical step, one that can crush any desire to innovate. When our instinct kicks in, it can block our mental faculties to the point that we cannot see beyond the problem. If we do not get past this stage, we may turn into a "deer in the headlights". Frozen in the "flight or fight" mode, the problem quickly fills up our vision of reality and hijacks our ability to see beyond it. No amount of reasoning or rational conversation is helpful as long as we are stuck in this layer.

Physical Intelligence is paramount to manifest any innovation into the material world. However, if we cannot expand our awareness and connect to subtle layers, we are driven only by the will to survive. In such a state of awareness, innovation is sourced from our fears and those fears are what will manifest into reality. At this layer, innovation is nothing more than a reaction to external triggers aimed at taking us back to safety. To go past our fears, we must learn to bypass the amygdala - sometimes just introducing a tiny pause does the work - so we can enable higher levels of innovative thinking. Dealing with our primitive emotions is the key factor to move to the next step of the journey.

# Social Intelligence gets us Beyond the Departure Threshold

The crossing of the departure threshold is an emotionally charged moment, one in which we define our relationship with the challenge and its stakeholders. Even if we may share the same objective reality, we all have a unique subjective experience of the challenge. Our emotions act like filters that shape the reality that we experience and on which we base our decisions, no matter how much thinking we will put into the challenge. Feelings are vital for any decisions; they point us in the proper direction, where we can put our logic at work.

Living our lives, we gather many experiences. Some are good, others are painful. Our limbic system uses our emotions to learn how to repeat the former ones and avoid the latter. This database of emotions is activated when we face a challenge, and it shapes how we see the reality of it. That is why we need to become fully aware of our relationship to the challenge we are facing.

Only when we become aware of our emotions and our relationship to the challenge, can we properly act on them. To accomplish that, we need to engage the faculties of the Orange layer: Social Intelligence helps us work with our emotions and create the connections we need to move forward in the journey.

At this layer, typically two solutions become visible; good or bad, yes or no, black or white, left or right, stay or leave, Democrat or Republican, do or die, in or out. If we cannot push beyond this duality, we will come out with innovations aimed at pleasing those within our sphere of concern more than those really addressing the challenge. To move past this limitation is to develop the ability to understand and share the feelings of another, so that we can combine all perspectives and fully understand the complexity of the challenge we are facing. It is only then that the outside challenge or problem to solve becomes personal to us, the inner and outer worlds synchronise, giving us the why-power we need to cross the departure threshold.

With this why-power, we can meet the opposing force of *gravity* that attempts to pull us back to the status quo before the beginning of the Innovator's Journey, to the safety of our comfort zone. To win over the force of gravity, we must remove everything unnecessary, all the layers of conditioning that make us heavy and keep us down.

Our inner beliefs, habits, and environment continuously cooperate to create and keep a working equilibrium in our lives. Those same forces that have established our current balance will work to pull us back from the

Departure Act any time we try to change for better or worse. Through a process of slowing down and subtraction, we can gently pull away from the traction of the status quo and allow for us to cross the departure threshold.

# How Cognitive Intelligence Enables the Apprenticeship

The first "breakthroughs" in the Departure Act emerge when we step outside the binary mindset of the previous step and we begin assessing the challenge from a broader perspective.

By unlocking the faculties of the Yellow layer and tapping into our Cognitive Intelligence, we begin to understand the complexity of reality beyond the typical two solutions. Accessing our database of previous experiences and knowledge, we can recognise patterns. Connections become visible, and we are able to step into the 'space in between' and see a third way to the typical problems of life.

The need to know and understand more drives us. Through the collection and combination of data, information and memories, and the acquisition of new knowledge and competencies, we can reframe the challenge through a more comprehensive model. It is akin to expanding our senses so that new dimensions and facets become visible, and we can make sense of things. This collective sense-making translates into models and maps through which our rational mind explains the past and the present, and predicts the future.

Predicting the future is the main purpose of our Cognitive Intelligence. That is why we love maps and models. The human brain is a prediction machine[39], always assessing what is going on around us to predict what will happen next. We work better when it knows what is coming. For our cognitive minds, "probable" is more appealing than "possible", answers are better than questions.

However, as we know the map is not the territory, and unless we find the strength to move beyond the realm of probability and embrace what is possible, we will never be able to create disruptive innovations. To move to the next level of creativity we need to embrace the power of questions and let them do the work, taking us beyond the boundaries of what we know and into uncharted territories.

## Intuitive Intelligence Feeds our Vision Quest

A known experiment consists of giving someone a paperclip asking to think of as many uses as possible for it. According to Sir Ken Robinson, most adults can think of ten to fifteen different uses for a paper clip, whereas kids typically come up with over a hundred alternative solutions.

When we uncondition our mind, we can make it go in infinite directions. Because of the unconditioned state in which kids are often in, they

---

[39] "The human brain, it is being increasingly argued in the scientific literature, is best viewed as an advanced prediction machine. By this view, the sophistication with which brains perceive and act upon the world has evolved to minimise the amount of surprise, or unpredictability experienced in a particular situation." - S. Chennu, V. Noreika, D. Gueorguiev, A. Blenkmann, S. Kochen, A. Ibáñez, A. M. Owen, and T. A. Bekinschtein. *Expectation and attention in hierarchical auditory prediction. The Journal of Neuroscience*, 33(27):11194–11205, 2013.

see space everywhere. In that expansive state, they can access infinite solutions to any problem. Paul Lindley, in *Little Wins: The Huge Power of Thinking Like a Toddler* put it perfectly when he said: "while a toddler's world might be geographically tiny, it is mentally limitless; conversely, when we grow up, we have the potential freedom to explore everything around us, but will often limit ourselves to the same narrow range of places, people and experiences."

As humans, our knowledge can be incredibly vast, but our minds are mostly limited by our conditioning, and so it sets the boundaries to what we envision. While as adults, we are conditioned to think that the answers must be found within what we know, kids have no such limitations. Their unconditioned state makes them immensely creative. They reside in a state where their mind spans infinite degrees of freedom.

When we can access the Blue layer, we awaken our Intuitive Intelligence and explore the land of possibilities, beyond what can be predicted. The key to unlock this layer of awareness, and the power of our intuition with it, lies in letting go of the need to know and open up to breakthrough and insightful questions.

Rainer Maria Rilke puts it best when he writes; "Have patience with everything that remains unsolved in your heart. Try to love the questions themselves, like locked rooms, or books written in a foreign language. Do not now look for the answers. They cannot now be given to you, because you would not be able to live them. And the point is, to live everything. Live the questions now. Perhaps then, someday far in the future, you will gradually, without even noticing it, live your way into the answer."

With everything we know and do not know about the challenge laid down before us, we stop doing and we just be, allowing for the questions to do their work. At this point of the Innovator's Journey, we have moved from the Ordinary World, where everything is measurable and can be understood and modelled, to the Mystical World, where everything is more subtle and elusive.

We may feel inner division, question ourselves and the whole journey, our logical mind might even pull us back into the Ordinary World. As overwhelming as this moment might be, it is only by having faith and staying with the questions that the vision for the way forward will emerge from the not-knowing.

# Spiritual Intelligence
# Informs the Revelation

Once the vision appears, it is tempting to jump straight to the implementation. Our human desire to make an impact, or to activate change, can quickly push us toward actions. Though, it would be like getting to the top of a mountain without taking the time to breath-in the moment.

The step of revelation is one of stillness. A timeless pause in our journey when we expand our senses beyond ourselves and open up to the wisdom of the Universe. That is the experience of *flow* that emerges from being in the Violet layer, a moment of complete connection in which separation dissolves. It is a space where we are the stream and within it at the same time. When we experience this moment of wholeness, we suddenly know something as if it came out of nowhere. As if it is part of who we are. Such is the work of Spiritual Intelligence.

In this realm, we are no longer creating the solution, but we become the channel through which the solution finds its way into the world. Until now, we may have been on a journey to reach a destination, from this moment on, we walk to fulfil our destiny; realising our full potential as Being Innovators.

The sages refer to this as a state of transcendence and intentioning, one in which we move from the 'solution' mindset, which is a reactive state, to the possibilities state, one which is choiceful and creative. Being in that space of pure inspiration and flow is a magical experience, almost addictive—an overwhelming feeling of possibilities and creative joy.

This realm, the step of Revelation, is the peak of the Innovator's Journey, and it is easy to lose ourselves in that heady space, and forget about opening up to receive the Boon, the next step in the Innovator's Journey. Remember, we are not innovating if we do not deliver the Boon into the Ordinary World. We are not creating the impact that is paramount for innovation.

To avoid that from happening, we must continuously remember our unifying intent; the reason why we started the journey in the first place. Our intent is birthed by our Spiritual Intelligence and serves as an invisible cord keeping us connected to the reality we share with all humanity.

# Intuitive Intelligence Unveils the Boon

Our Intuitive Intelligence is the one that understands and translates the language of the Universe into human ideas, images, or thoughts. It allows us to read the omen, and what was once invisible becomes visible. Possibilities manifest themselves around us. Do they arise because we unleash our Intuitive Intelligence, or were they there all the time and only now can we notice them?

In the end, it makes no difference. What really matters is that when we unlock the faculties of the Blue layer, we can move energy from the realm of infinite possibilities into the realm of probabilities. We are finally rewarded with the Boon.

Most of the time, the Boon is still undefined and elusive, and it may be hard to describe it or give it a shape. It is more like a seed that must be planted and nourished. Some may sprout quickly; others may take a while. Love and care are fundamental to allow the Boon to bloom into a formed idea; something with a shape that can be represented with words and symbols so that our cognitive mind can grasp it and reflect upon it.

Many innovation journeys die at this point. The intuition is often so disruptive that self-doubts creep in. The more the idea is ground-breaking, the bigger the doubts. If we give in to these doubts, they could trigger self-preservation reactions that can undermine our journey. We could lose trust in our own intuition. We might hide or become impatient, thus wasting its potential. Receiving the Boon involves mastering these inner demons.

We cannot measure intuition the same way we measure a well-formed idea. Intuition is nothing more than a feeble and trembling flame that can die out at the first blow. If we can keep it alive however, we can use it to ignite the power of all the other faculties. The key to move past the doubts and forward in the journey is to find meaning in our endeavour. When we recognise that there is a purpose bigger than ourselves in the Boon, we are able to overcome the fear of not knowing, and we find the strength to invest our energy in a far distant and still unclear outcome. In the end, is it not this what we do when we plant the seed of a tree, even if we know that the fruits are far ahead in time, or we may never enjoy its fruits?

# Cognitive Intelligence
# Leads the Road Back

When we engage our Cognitive Intelligence in service of the Boon, we begin to create a structure for the flame lit in the Mystical World to rage into fire. This step constitutes our return to the Ordinary World, where our imagination acts as a catalyst, activating our skills and knowledge to shape the configuration needed to move our vision from probability to reality.

On the road back, our Cognitive Intelligence helps us with understanding and making sense of things. We see and form connections, evolve systems, and define metrics and goals. Cognitive Intelligence makes concepts relatable for others and helps us build strategies to break through the resistance imposed by the Ordinary World.

In this leg of the Innovator's Journey, we will meet resistance. The more our ideas gain substance, the more they will activate opposing forces. These forces can take many forms such as a cognitive bias, the NIMBY syndrome (not in my back yard), the fear of change of individuals and groups trapped in a self-preservation mindset and culture.

Spiritual and Intuitive intelligences express their potential only in the here and now. They are unbounded by time and space. Only when our cognitive mind comes into play, past and future are invited to the journey. We bridge what we know with what we do not know. We compare the vision in our head with the reality of the world around us.

And when these two are not aligned, it is easy to think that we must be wrong. When our subjective world and what we believe to be the objective one do not align, it is more comfortable to deem that the subjective one must be wrong. We might second guess our imagination. We might begin to question or even sabotage our ideas and ourselves. The same Cognitive Intelligence that empowers our intuitions can crush them in a moment.

The way forward lies in experimentation, prototyping and play. The models we conceive helps others evaluate our idea and buy into our imagination. We also learn and expand our worldly skills and knowledge so that we can add substance to our intuition. And because our Cognitive Intelligence is driven by performances and metrics, at this step, the clarity and concreteness we experience triggers within us a sense of momentum. We feel exciting accelerations and moments of elation.

# Social Intelligence and the Return Threshold

"We achieve results in life not because we are objective but because we care." In his book, *Liminal Thinking*, Dave Gray reminds us that what inspires people to act towards any goal is their emotional connection with that goal. This is particularly true when what we want to create is a change. And innovation is, by definition, all about change. The more unpredictable and unexpected the change, or the more disruptive the innovation, the more important it is to be aware of the connection of all stakeholders to our innovation.

Change, particularly when we move from the known into the unknown, can be frightening and unpleasant, triggering a wide range of contrasting emotions within ourselves and others. These emotions have the power to fuel or crash the innovation journey of manifestation. They can harness the individual and collective energy needed to bring our ideas out there in the world. Or they can trigger fear-based thoughts that raise barriers and trap us in the safety of the familiar status quo.

The impact that we want to create is on the other side of this vital threshold. One that requires a great amount of energy to cross. Energy that we can harness through the faculties of the Orange layer so that we can infuse it into our ideas. Energy to give strength to our own actions but also to engage others. When others resonate with our energy, our power is amplified, we expand the locus of our intention, and we maximize the impact of our actions. We are then ready to deliver the Boon to the world.

# Physical Intelligence Informs the Return with the Boon

This is the last step of the Innovator's Journey. For innovation to have an impact, it must fully manifest into the material world. That does not mean it has to be a physical product, though it must create an impact on our shared reality. This is where we need to rely on the Physical Intelligence of the Red layer. Without it, it is impossible to complete the manifestation journey, and any innovation will fail to deliver any impact.

At this step we realize our journey to fully become a Being Innovator. And along with us, the innovation we have nurtured for so long becomes a thing of its own. Connected, yet separated from us. The energy from which our innovation has been sourced finds its form in the Ordinary World. Our configuration is now in full manifestation.

This moment is as much generative as it is often messy and chaotic, as with anything that comes into manifestation in the material world.

"Babies are born in blood and chaos; stars and galaxies come into being amid the release of massive primordial cataclysms," muses Steve Pressfield. Our primal instinct to survive emerges amidst the chaos, messiness, and hardships of reality.

"Will my innovation survive out there?" Our ego asks.

As we know from the sages, ego is the organ of manifestation, and its main task is to keep our soul and body, our awareness and configuration, together. Because when they get separated, we are no more.

It is easy to get overwhelmed by our ego's instinct of survival and become unable to see beyond our fears. Everything can become a "fight, flight, or freeze" situation. This instinct has been hardwired into our brains over millions of years of evolution. Our amygdala, where distrust and fear reside, reacts to external triggers way faster than our prefrontal cortex.

However, when we reconnect with the intention we have been gifted with, we become infused with a new sense of inevitability and peace. We have found new strength to endure and overcome the failures and the struggles of the Innovator's Journey, as in the lives of Gandhi and Dyson. We can now celebrate the arrival of the Being Innovator.

# Integration Moment

The Innovator's Journey ensues when we expand our awareness, triggering an inner journey as much as an outer one. Rarely linear and straightforward, it is, in fact, messy and chaotic, with thrilling accelerations and abrupt stops, rewarding successes and painful fallbacks.

Only by accessing a subtler level of awareness, the faculties we need to proceed are unlocked. This happens through a process that requires the subtraction of our conditioning. However, it is a process that can cause strong duality within when we shift from the Ordinary World to the Mystical one and back. This duality is part of the tension and emotions that help us understand where we are on our own Innovator's Journey.

Rage, frustration, bitterness, resentment, and anger signal that we are somewhere in the Departure Act. Inner division, resignation, sometimes despair, hopelessness, surrendering in the not-knowing, momentary bursts of elation and then depression, are all typical of the Initiation Act. Euphoria, elation, a sense of momentum, restless energy taking us forward, bliss, forgiveness, gratitude, and infinite possibilities manifest in the Arrival Act.

For those seeking to discover more dimensions of the self or harness breakthrough innovations, following the Innovator's Journey's is a crucial exercise.

The following table summarises the faculties needed to move through each step of the journey. You will also find some questions that can help you in your own journey.

| STEP | INTELLIGENCE | SELF INQUIRIES |
| --- | --- | --- |
| The call to adventure | Physical | Am I in danger? Should I run from the threat or face it? Is this my challenge? |
| Crossing the departure threshold | Social | What emotions are awakened by this situation? What is my relationship with the challenge? Where is the energy coming from? |
| The apprenticeship | Cognitive | What do I know about this challenge? What do I don't know about this challenge? What do I need to learn? |
| The vision quest | Intuitive | What is this challenge telling or asking me? What is the big picture here? |
| The revelation | Spiritual | What is my calling? What new reality is ready to emerge through me? Why me? Who am I in this journey? |
| The Boon | Intuitive | What is the purpose of this Boon? What impact can this Boon create? |
| The road back | Cognitive | How do I know that this idea makes sense? What can I do to prove to myself that this idea works? What do I need to make it work? |
| Crossing the arrival threshold | Social | What energy is needed to realize the potential of this idea? How do I engage others in my journey? |
| Return with the Boon | Physical | What work needs to be done? What are the next steps? |

# 3.3 The Pitfalls of Bypassing the Innovator's Journey



Many journeys never reach the final step. The innovator gets derailed at some point of the journey, the Boon goes lost, and no impact is created. Only when we get to the end of the Innovator's Journey is a boundless innovation fully manifested, thus making an impact. The magnitude of that impact, both in depth and width, depends on how far we get in the Innovator's Journey, and consequently, how many faculties we have unlocked and integrated.

We do not need to walk the whole journey to innovate. At any point in the Departure Act, we can jump into manifestation, bypassing part of the journey. However, by doing so we will not have engaged all our faculties and unleashed all our intelligences, thus mostly creating incremental innovations or delivering lower impact. That is not optimal, however in certain situations that might be precisely what we need.

A similar phenomenon can be observed when we attempt to innovate within the layer that we are confined to. Due to our existing conditioning and blocks, our faculties may have been hijacked by the shadow-side of one layer, unable to access the other layers and their faculties. Or due to the effort involved in the process of subtraction - which requires us to look inwards and challenge our own beliefs - we may decide that it is easier to bypass the journey and move horizontally, rushing into execution. When that happens, our ability to progress through the steps of the Innovator's Journey is hindered, and our potential to innovate is limited.

Even if we unlock all the layers and access the subtle and causal realms of the self, thus opening a channel to the *causal library*, we may fail in delivering the boundless innovations we aspire for. In fact, accessing the faculties of all five layers is only half the story. That constitutes the upward arc of the Innovator's Journey. However, it is only when we embrace the second half of the journey that we fully integrate the faculties of all five layers and transform the potential of our wholistic intelligence. Then we can source the doing from the being and turn it into boundless innovation.

In the next five chapters, we will examine in great details the pitfalls of being stuck in any one layer.

# Primitive Response of
# Fight, Flight or Freeze

*No power so effectually robs the mind of all its*
*powers of acting and reasoning as fear.*
Edmund Burke

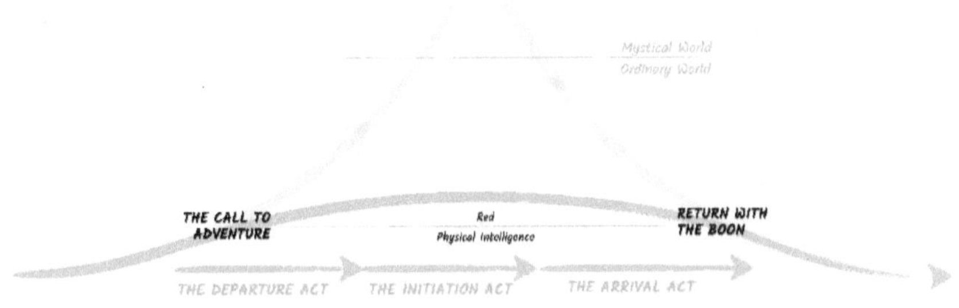


Over a decade ago, in 2008, the world went through the worst financial crisis since the Great Depression of 1929. Felt by many individuals and almost every industry, the raw materials sector was hit particularly hard as shrinking economies meant shrinking production, which meant less need for raw materials. This in turn led to the price of raw materials rising dramatically, hitting somewhere close to $120 dollars per barrel of oil.

Procter & Gamble (P&G), a company which relied heavily on such raw materials quickly went into damage limitation mode. One employee at the time noted how the metaphor of "weathering the storm" was broadcast widely by leaders within the company. It was, as with many organizations at the time, hands on deck – peace is on the horizon, even if it was not clear as to when yet. For many customers on the ground too, the realities of the recession were hard pills to swallow. P&G in response to this crisis was celebrated for lowering their prices, but the fact of the matter was much different.

"In July of 2009, Procter & Gamble executives made clear that prices in some markets would be reduced to account for currency changes, but that the net impact would be that prices would stay higher than they were before the recession hit," mentions Fortune. Instead of looking after their customers, they instead attempted to broaden their market share through price-shift strategies that often hid the real costs of their products.

Did such a move work? By mid-2009, P&G reported profits of $2.5 billion, down 18% from a year earlier. Sales of its products — which include such brands as Bounty paper towels and Tide detergent — were down 11%.

***

When faced with a challenge, real or imagined, the first reaction of most of us is the need to survive.

Survival is the motive of the Red layer. Together with materialization, ensuring our survival is another task of Physical Intelligence. And it is an important one. If we lose our configuration - our form - we are no more of this world, and we indeed cannot innovate.

However, when we get stuck in the survival loop, we become obsessed with the form. Every event is perceived as a potential threat, and preserving ourselves becomes the only purpose of our efforts. All our actions tend to be a reaction to something, more than being creative actions from choice. This is the nature of the shadow-side of the Red layer.

Like that of many others, the P&G story shows that in times of crisis, the attitude towards risks changes: perspectives, hopes and vision get diminished. In nature, prey often have the shortest vision and scope, nibbling on the grassy ground. At the same time, they have a heightened alertness, and their instinct is conditioned towards self-preservation. We humans are not much different. According to Dr Lisa Feldman Barrett's work, our brain is a super-efficient predicting machine dedicated to keeping our body alive and healthy.

Most humans and organizations in similar settings act out in primitive ways; out of fear, most of their actions aim at protecting their status quo. Bypassing the Innovator's Journey, their goal is to find the quickest way to fix the immediate threat.

Security, paying our bills, taking care of our daily needs, etc., become the key drivers of our lives when we are hijacked by the shadow-side of the Red layer. Our main concerns are our - and our dear ones' - short-term. Whether at work or in our family, we are motivated by (self) preservation. Saving and having enough reserves for a "rainy day" becomes important to us. Where others do not see a reason to worry, we will feel inclined to worry.

When an organization or ecosystem is operating out of the shadow-side of the Red layer, it results in high pressure and stressful environments. We notice intense micromanagement focused on results, with little tolerance for mistakes in such a world, and an "up or out" culture driven by fierce competition, opportunism, and territorial ambitions.

Without space for thought or reflection, it becomes impossible for an entity stuck in the shadow of the Red layer to view itself as part of a larger whole. Instead, it may continue to march onward with no higher plan, focusing on the short-term and smaller picture. This might explain how P&G lost sight of the suffering of its customers.

In the shadow of the Red layer, we tend to shun ideas from the outside and become harbourers of the Not-Invented-Here Syndrome: "if others come into this research, they will take credit for it. I might lose my job. I might lose my promotion, my bonus – my status".

In the literal sense of the word, to be in a self-preservation mode is to design our behaviours around the need to keep ourselves away from death and destruction. Yet when put next to the old maxim, "what doesn't kill you makes you stronger" it is clear that this is a mindset which impedes personal growth.

Fears of scarcity are also misplaced. The fear of not getting enough, of lacking, of scarcity, is deeply ingrained in our societies due to a long history of war, disease, and famine. In 1962, James Neel, a geneticist at the University of Michigan, proposed the thrifty gene hypothesis, positing that evolutionary pressures in the form of food scarcity throughout human history led to the selection of thrifty genes. These genes predispose to metabolic thrift to protect against famine's detrimental impact on survival and reproductive fitness.

For a time then, our fear of scarcity was well-placed. It helped natural selection in facilitating the survival of our species during times of scarcity. However, we are speaking about diasporas and ice ages which occurred thousands upon thousands of years ago. Fortunately, for many, starvation is more unlikely than ever before in history. Yet this primal instinct still remains, and it is only by expanding awareness that we can overcome it properly.

The above instinct explains P&G's reaction to the crisis. Operating out of the shadow-side of the Red layer, it is understandable why self-preservation was an important priority for P&G during the economic reality of 2008. When we interpret such a time as a potential threat, preserving the form becomes the only purpose of our actions, thus limiting our potential to innovate.

What the story of P&G shows is that no matter how successful we are, if we get stuck in the primitive survival state, it becomes difficult to expand our awareness and progress further on the Innovator's Journey. Subsequently, innovation and success quickly slip away. Rediscovering the emotional connection with the stakeholders and society at large is the first step to move beyond fears and infuse new energy into our innovations' efforts.

# The Feel-Good Conundrum
# of Innovation

*The inner conformist is stronger*
*than the inner activist*
Michael Morris

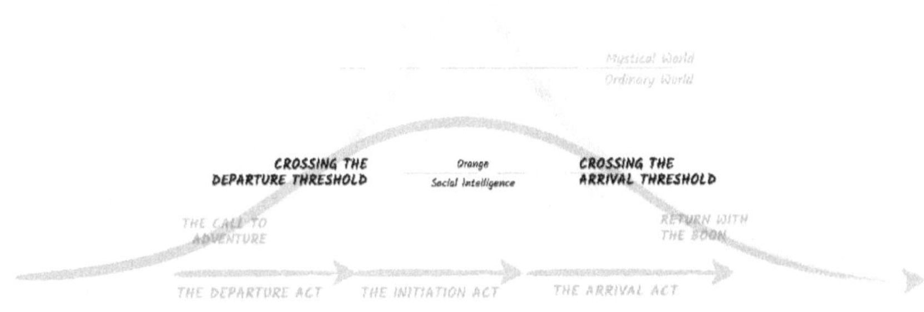


If you come across a photograph from any time in the previous century, the odds are that you have in your hand a photograph taken with a Kodak camera, with Kodak film, on Kodak paper, and with Kodak technology. Kodak, once known as Eastman Kodak, was a true pioneer of film and digital photography and was the brainchild of George Eastman and Henry A.

Strong, who founded the company on September 4, 1888.

Eastman trademarked the word "Kodak" because he liked the sound of it. In his own words: "The letter 'K' had been a favourite with me — it seemed a strong, incisive sort of letter." Eastman was a man with strong feelings on trademarks in general: "A trademark should be short." It should be "vigorous," and it should be "incapable of being misspelt to an extent that will destroy its identity." Most of all, though, a trademark "must mean nothing."

When coming up with Kodak, it was simply a game of alphabet soup, albeit a bit more inspired. Eastman tried out hundreds of permutations and eventually settled with a name that would become one of the biggest brands of the next one hundred years.

By 1966 combined sales of all Kodak units surpassed $4 billion, and Kodak employment exceeded 100,000. 30 years later, it would be laying off over 15% of its staff and witnessing a share-value decline of almost 50% (from $93 to $53) in the space of one year.

So what happened? What stopped the company who had developed film for the NASA moon landings from continuing its march through the annals of history? In a word, themselves.

In Mary Shelley's *Frankenstein* (1818), Victor Frankenstein was a scientist who wanted to create life itself. He stitches together parts from the dead bodies of criminals executed at the gallows and brings his creation to life during an electrical storm. The monster subsequently scares Frankenstein as it begins to kill without reason or cause. Frankenstein then chases the monster to the Arctic and dies in pursuit of the creature. The monster then follows by killing himself out of grief.

Nearly 100 years later, in 1975, one Steve Sasson, an engineer at Eastman Kodak, would go on to create the company's own monster by inventing the world's first digital camera.

In 1976, Kodak had an 85% market share in cameras and a 90% market share in the film. In 1973, 120,000 people were employed by Kodak. By 2011, the number had dropped to 18,800. Between 2003 and 2011, their share price dropped by over 90%. By 2012, after 124 years in business, they went bankrupt. Over the course of over a century, Kodak had created, and subsequently lost, an entire ecosystem of innovation. Despite having invented the world's first digital camera.

What can be learned from it?

Kodak was working from a mindset that saw a tool for progress as the monster under the bed, a monster which could be fed piecemeal and would leave them alone. In the eighties, Vince Barabba, at that time Kodak's head of market intelligence, was asked to conduct an extensive research effort that looked at the core technologies and likely adoption curves around silver halide film versus digital photography.

The results of the study were twofold. First of all, it established that digital photography had the potential capability to replace Kodak's established film-based business. The second important finding was that it would take some time for that to occur and that Kodak had roughly ten years to prepare for the transition – and prepare it did not.

The study's projections took into account numerous factors: the cost of digital photography equipment, the quality of images and prints, and the interoperability of various components, such as cameras, displays, and printers. All factors pointed to the conclusion that adoption of digital photography would be minimal and would not threaten their business for about a decade. The coming years would prove the study's theories to be remarkably accurate, both in the short and long term. They knew what was going to happen, yet they did little or nothing to prepare for it.

When George Fisher became the CEO of Kodak in 1993, he told the New York Times that Kodak "regarded digital photography as the enemy, an evil juggernaut that would kill the chemical-based film and paper business that fueled Kodak's sales and profits for decades". This emotive, exclamatory declaration of war against the very product the company had created almost two decades prior may seem odd, especially since it would be Fisher himself who would go on to rally the troops and aggressively invest more than $2 billion in R&D for digital imaging three years later. However, what this quote shows is an emotional attachment to the old world and a profound misunderstanding of the new one–fear of change of the status quo and loyalty to a bygone era.

It was this emotional weight around Kodak's neck that would repeatedly prove to be its undoing. Before Mark Zuckerberg wrote a line of Facebook's code, Kodak made a prescient purchase, acquiring a photo-sharing site called Ofoto in 2001. The company missed its chance and failed to embrace its historical tagline of "share memories, share life." Instead of becoming a pioneer of a new category called social networking – wherein people could share pictures, personal updates, and links to news and information – Kodak used Ofoto to try to get more people to print digital images. Dogmatic in their conviction that what they knew and owed so much of their livelihood too would triumph regardless of the facts.

The company sold the site to *Shutterfly* as part of its bankruptcy plan for less than $25 million in April 2012. That same month, Facebook plunked down $1 billion to acquire Instagram, the 13-employee company Systrom had co-founded 18 months earlier.

***

The Orange Layer is driven by our Social Intelligence. The faculties of this layer play a crucial role both in the Departure and the Arrival Acts of the Innovator's Journey. They allow us to build a personal connection with the challenge and also to become aware of the impact of our creative work on our ecosystem. This awareness can infuse passion into our work, but if we cannot harness this passion to engage the other layers, we may end up stuck in a feel-good mindset.

This feel-good mindset is the shadow side of the Orange layer that makes it essential for us to belong, whether it is at work, at home, or in the groups we are part of. This shadow side pushes us to make an effort to be an important part of the collective and go out of our way to please others so that we are acknowledged.

When the need to be accepted is the most important driver of an individual or the collective, looking forward to anything but the short-term is impossible. Groupthink prevails, and the desire for harmony or conformity pushes the group to agree at all costs, subordinating both logic and uniqueness. We see the emergence of the Abilene paradox[40], where members of an ecosystem make decisions that are counter to the interests of all of them.

When we are operating from the shadow side of the Orange layer, we are unable to see beyond the duality of any challenge; "*does it make us/me feel good or not?*" From such a space, only feel-good innovations can arise. Everything that challenges the collective's harmony or conformity is quickly ignored or dismissed.

Just look at Kodak's story. They created the digital camera, invested in the technology, and even understood that photos would be shared online. Where they failed was in realizing that online photo sharing was the new business and not the expansion of the printing business they had

---

[40] The term  Abilene Paradox" was introduced by Jerry B. Harvey in a 1974 article. Harvey opens his article with an anecdote about a family that drove for more than 50 miles to have dinner in the town of Abilene. A dinner that nobody in the family wanted, but they all said yes without sharing their real feelings for fear of seeming insensitive. Source:  Jerry B. Harvey, *The abilene paradox: The management of agreement, Organizational Dynamics*, Volume 3, Issue 1, 1974, Pages 63-80, ISSN 0090-2616, https://doi.org/10.1016/0090-2616(74)90005-9.

loved for so long. If Kodak had not been so unconsciously trapped in its emotional connection with its own story and had incorporated the other intelligences into their way of thinking, then perhaps logic and facts would have aided their cause.

Instead, Kodak became so clouded by its attachment to its story and by its need to feel good that it stopped asking what its business stood for and what it could do for its consumers; instead, it retreated into a fortress of emotional certainty, one from which it would never escape.

To grow, those locked in the shadow side of the Orange layer must awaken a deeper level of self and ecosystemic awareness, create safe environments for addressing the "elephant in the room", and practice speaking up. This will galvanize innovators, build their self-esteem, and create a new level of harmony that makes space for the uniqueness of the individuals to shine instead of enhancing the feel-good culture of conformity within the ecosystem.

Such developments create massive levels of empowerment but also can lead to attrition, tension, and conflict as old paradigms are broken down. Yet it is through this pain that innovators find the courage to step out of the shadow side of the Orange layer and advance further on their Innovator's Journey, and subsequently make it possible to liberate more innovation potential.

# The Need-Proof Loop of
# Seasoned Innovators

*In God we trust, all others must bring data.*
W. Edwards Deming

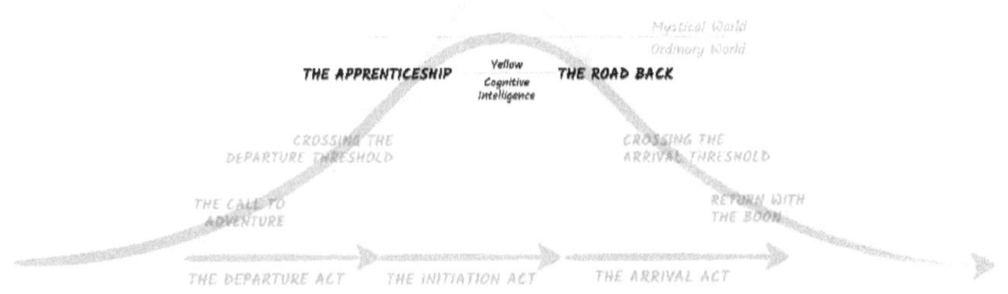


With Nokia, it all started with the "1011". It was by no means the first commercially available mobile phone and it was not the first GSM handset, but it was the first mass-produced GSM phone. It did little more than make calls and send text, but it was all Nokia needed to build a worldwide empire. In October 1998, Nokia became the best-selling mobile phone brand in the world, with their profits totalling $1 billion in 1995 and growing to almost $4 billion by 1999.

Unlike Kodak, Nokia did not set up its own gallows. Instead, it was its inability to balance its five layers in any feasible way, reinforced by overwhelming reliance – backed up by solid sales all the way until the end – on previous successes and by the fact that no-one inside their configuration could envision something better.

Historically, Nokia had been a surprisingly adaptive company, moving in and out of many different businesses—paper, electricity, rubber galoshes.

For years, the company had been a conglomerate, with a number of disparate businesses operating under the Nokia umbrella. In the early nineteen-nineties, anticipating the rise of cellphones, executives got rid of everything but the telecom business. Even more strikingly, Nokia was hardly a technological laggard—on the contrary, it came up with its first smartphone, the Communicator, back in 1996, and had built a prototype of a touch-screen, Internet-enabled phone at the end of the nineties. It also spent enormous amounts of money on research and development.

It is more accurate to say that Nokia was, at its heart, a hardware company rather than a software company – that is, its engineers were experts in building physical devices, but not the programs that make those devices work. In the end, the company profoundly underestimated the importance of software, including the apps that run on smartphones, to the experience of using a phone, as what they saw to have worked in the past by all estimations should continue to work again. Nokia's development process was long dominated by hardware engineers while software experts were marginalized. This misunderstanding of the importance of integration seems more illogical now, however back then the link between intersectionality and innovation was much less well-known. It is noteworthy that Apple, in stark contrast, saw hardware and software as equally important parts of a whole; they encouraged employees to work in multidisciplinary teams to design their – much more successful – products.

It was not just that Nokia failed to recognize the increasing importance of software, though. It also underestimated how important the transition to smartphones would be. And this was, in retrospect, a classic case of a company being enthralled (and, in a way, imprisoned) by its past success. Nokia was, after all, earning more than fifty percent of all the profits in the mobile-phone industry in 2007, and most of those profits were not coming from smartphones. Diverting a lot of resources into a high-end, low-volume business (which is what the touch-screen smartphone business was in 2007) would have seemed illogical.

Frank Nuovo, former Vice President and Chief of Design at Nokia, when speaking to the *Australian Financial Review* in 2013, had this to say: "I look back and I think Nokia was just a very big company that started to maintain its position more than innovate for new opportunities." Instead of dreaming big and adopting blue-sky thinking and future vision, Nokia was looking at short-term ends based upon a tried and tested formula.

Its confidence in its approach would ultimately be the crux of the giant's downfall. Tricia Wang, an ethnographic researcher working for Nokia in 2009 highlighted the brand's overindulgence in what could be measured.

As part of her work, Wang spent years working in various jobs in China to ascertain what consumers want in the Middle Kingdom. From living with migrants to living in internet cafés to working as a street vendor, Wang discovered that, despite Nokia's own data, many indicators showed that low-income consumers were ready to pay for more expensive smartphones.

These findings, Wang notes years later in an article for online ethnography magazine Ethnography Matters, went very much against the data dogma within Nokia's walls. As Wang writes: "I reported my findings and recommendations to headquarters. But Nokia did not know what to do with my findings. They said my sample size of 100 was weak and small compared to their sample size of several million data points." Even more tellingly of the problem at hand, "they [Nokia] said that there weren't any signs of my insights in their existing datasets."

This was because the previous datasets - at this point Nokia's gospel - were so quantitative that they were incapable of finding the nuances of culture on the ground. This cultural blindspot, a potential innovation kick-starter, went unseen, and is one of many of Nokia's own organisational shortcomings that saw its castle reveal itself to be built on sand.

By 2007 Steve Jobs and Apple were the future, not Nokia. "That is a pain point for me, because by far they didn't invent the touch screen phone, we had applications, we had internet phones, we had all that functionality...but all of our user testings pointed to the fact that no-one wanted touch phones." As Frank Nuovo words highlight, Nokia was held hostage by its logical way of thinking, and even when they realised that this could well be the future, they failed to act. "We realised at Nokia that touch was increasingly important and were working towards doing it, but when a company is really busy holding on to what it has built, it is difficult to put enough of a push towards something so drastically new and engender urgency in it."

In the same interview, Nuovo admitted that "Nokia became more of a maintainer, more of an iterator, whereas innovation only comes in re-invention and Nokia waited too long to make the next big bold move".

And they made another mistake. Nokia overestimated the strength of its brand, and believed that even if it was late to the smartphone game it would be able to catch up quickly. Long after the iPhone's release, in fact, Nokia continued to insist that its superior hardware designs would win over users, as that was what had worked before. In 2008, Nokia was said to have one of the most valuable brands in the world. But it failed to recognize that brands today are not as resilient as they once were. Consumers are now expecting constant innovation; when companies fall behind, consumers are quick to punish them. Logical yet unimaginative, Nokia proved that the proof is in the next pudding, not the previous one.

***

As we have learned, the Yellow layer is the threshold between a more re-active mindset, ingrained in the grosser Red and Orange layers, and a more creative one that emerges from the subtler Blue and Violet layers. The Yellow layer is the layer that releases the power of our Cognitive Intelligence and its ability to connect data and reason to envision a third way. Most of the innovations shaping our world right now, from self-driving cars to AI systems, are enabled by our ability to process huge amounts of data and extract meaningful insights and knowledge from it. There are no doubts that our Cognitive Intelligence played a crucial role in humanity's achieve-ments, at least when it comes to innovation.

However, this astonishing collection of successes comes with its side-effects. One is the rising complexity of the challenges that innovations have created, as we described in chapter one. Another one is that our suc-cesses have often got us stuck in cognitive loops. The more successful we are, the more inclined we are to keep doing what has worked so far instead of seeking new ways. We become enthralled by the shiny shadow side of the Yellow layer.

The successes achieved through the sheer force of our cognitive abil-ities reinforce the idea that we can predict and determine the future if we have enough data, knowledge and skills. And when we are unable to do so, we prefer to blame a lack of skills or knowledge before anything else. We saw Nokia do this with Wang's research. We respond by increasing our effort to accumulate more knowledge, more data and more skills, with the conviction that this will allow us to push through the challenge and predict what is next.

And it works. Until it does not.

Most of the time, this mindset allows us to keep a steady and linear growth. Numbers and metrics allow us to keep everything under control, to make our plans work, and prove that we are capable of thinking our way into the future.

Then a disruption happens, one that shakes the industry and turns the market upside down. Such as the global pandemic of 2020 or the emergence of an outlier - like Apple did with the iPhone - that plays outside the boundaries of logic, known data and information. An event that challenges the perfect logic of the status quo. When all our energy is applied in using our Cognitive Intelligence, and something like that happens, we are caught off-guard. We react by digging in and further obsessing over data and facts. As Mike Tyson said, "everybody has a plan until they get punched in the mouth." This is how we react when we are in the shadow side of the Yellow layer.

Nokia's story shows us the risks of over-relying on our Cognitive Intelligence. When we are only driven by logic, we want proof before acting. We measure ourselves and our initiatives only by the ROI. We are not able to take the leap of faith beyond numbers, data and knowledge. We are enthralled by what we know.

The outcome is king, and data is the only thing we trust. For this reason, we act only when the probability of success (a typical rationale of a reasoning culture based on data) is high. We seek what is probable, and in doing so, we overlook or dismiss what is possible. This is understandable. Our brain is an advanced predicting machine, continuously assessing the environment against what it already knows, finding patterns to apply, and minimising the amount of surprise. But this attitude confines our ability to innovate to the boundaries of what we can know and understand, of what our predicting machine recognizes as achievable.

In *Willpower doesn't work*, Ben Hardy tells the insightful story of backflips in motocross. Until the '90s, doing a backflip with a motorbike was considered impossible. Then in 1998, a motocross film showed people attempting backflips off a ramp into the water. What was unthinkable only a few years before began to look possible for the first time, and many started looking for ways to do it. The first to succeed was Caleb Wyatt in 2002. His achievement redefined what was possible on a motorbike. Four years later, Travis Pastrana landed the first double backflip, and in 2015 Josh Sheehan delivered the first triple backflip. In 2014, ten years old Jasyn Roney became the youngest person to complete a backflip on a motorcycle. Was he better, smarter, more talented or passionate than the motocross riders in the '90s?

No, not really. The only difference is that in the '90s doing a backflip seemed physically impossible to our mind. Until someone broke free of that mental barrier and moved those boundaries. Roney grew up in a world where doing a backflip was the norm.

When we get hijacked by the shadow-side of the Yellow layer, our ability to innovate is hampered by the need to predict the outcomes and our inability to see beyond the boundaries of the known. It is clear that from this state, the innovation that can be generated is merely a predictable one. This can lead to some disruption because we are not bound by the need to feel good, but we are limited by our cognitive ability to figure them out in advance.

Until we seek the way forward in the data and knowledge from the past, we can not really make breakthrough advancements. It is only when someone breaks the boundaries of what is known and possible that we realise we can do more.

At the moment of writing this book, the world is dealing with a global pandemic that has caught most of humanity unprepared. Individuals and businesses all around the globe are facing huge challenges where their very own survival is at stake. One of the biggest challenges for everyone is our inability to calculate or predict the future, even the immediate one. We have a massive amount of data from the past, but nothing that can really help us figure out what is going to happen next. Individuals and organizations unable to rise past this state run the risk of becoming paralysed by such levels of uncertainty. This paralysis is a symptom of how we can be blindsided by the shadow side of the Yellow layer.

The secret then is to use curiosity as an enabler with which we attempt to break free from the shadow of the Yellow layer. We can advance on our Innovator's Journey by taking a leap of faith into subtler layers, engaging our Intuitive Intelligence to see what is possible beyond the probabilities. Nokia could have done that by using a more kidful, progressive way of experimenting instead of one based on protectionist conservatism.

Once new possibilities emerge from the subtler layers, we can bring these new ideas back into the space of logic where we can put our experiences and skills to good use and plan out the way forward.

Thankfully, an individual or environment operating predominantly from the Yellow layer needs only to become more aware of possibilities beyond the known and familiar, and go ahead and develop its access to the Intuitive Intelligence to crawl out of the shadow of the Yellow layer. By advancing on the Innovator's Journey and harnessing the complementary nature of the intuitive mind, an organization or ecosystem can once again become unafraid of failure, take risks, step beyond the status quo, and subsequently unleash its full innovation potential.

# Innovator's Drama: from Being Kidful to Being Childish

*'No artist tolerates reality,' says Nietzsche. That is
true, but no artist can get along without reality.*

Albert Camus

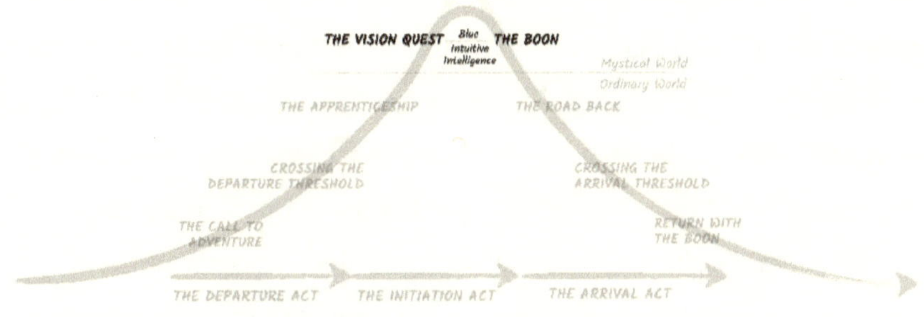


"*Men are on the moon*" were the first words in The Guardian printed on
21 July 1969. The event was the culmination of dreams which mankind
shared since the beginning of time, and the earth stood mesmerised by the
sheer brilliance of this benchmark moment in human innovation.

Almost 50 years later in 2018, NASA officials would announce that
America's next great space telescope and spiritual successor to the Hubble
Space Telescope, the James Webb Space Telescope, would not be ready in
spring 2019, as they had hoped. The reality was that engineers needed more
time to finish it, with their new deadline being two entire years later, in

2021. How the agency attributed with owning some of humanity's greatest technological feats could be a full two years off deadline, it turns out, would become very telling of its interior environment.

Tom Young, a highly respected engineer who has been involved with NASA since the 1970s was brought in to discover what had gone wrong. Apart from the usual suspect, human error, there was another, more intangible force at play: human optimism. The conclusion that Young came to was that the staggering schedule delays and cost overruns of the telescope were the result of "excessive optimism" from all levels of the team working on the project. From the mission's engineers through to the program managers, NASA was full to the brim with blue-sky thinking.

Envisioned in 1997 with a planned launch date of 2007 at a cost of $0.5 billion, the project is - at the moment of this writing - 14 years behind and exceeds initial price tag costs by almost $10 billion. This is, of course, not particularly good evidence of a strong business acumen at NASA, but it must not be forgotten that this is a project which aimed high, potentially being the world's most powerful space telescope upon completion.

Blue-sky thinking is essential for boundless innovation, and NASA is a company which has always been at the forefront of journeying into the unknown, skirting along the line between human ingenuity and the impossible. Optimism, then, was essential to NASA's success. This enthusiasm was crucial to the organization's success, but that is not to say that the possibility for problems caused by imbalance are not there.

"You have to be optimistic to beat gravity and to do the amazing things that NASA does," spoke Lori Garver, who served as the agency's deputy administrator from 2009 to 2013, to the Atlantic in 2018. "On the other hand, that has caused us to overpromise and make mistakes."

The most publicly known missions —the Hubble Space Telescope, the Mars Curiosity rover — launched into space well beyond their budget and timeline goals. This is true for several other missions since the agency's opening in 1958. This is in many ways the nature of the beast. When you are trying to do something no one else has done before, you do not always know how much work it will take.

Yet this optimism, especially for an agency funded by taxpayer money, must be grounded in reality to some extent. Else it will inevitably become a source of scrutiny, which it did. In 2012, the NASA office of the inspector general published a report titled, *NASA's Challenges to Meeting Cost, Schedule, and Performance Goals.*

The document was based on interviews with dozens of agency employees, including current and former administrators, the directors of various NASA facilities, and project managers. There were several major challenges, the report concluded, including an underestimation of technical complexity, funding instability, and shifting priorities from presidential administrations and Congress. And the top challenge, the report said, was NASA's positive outlook.

The report goes on to state that project managers were particularly "overly optimistic about how much effort developing and testing new technology will take". Paul Martin, speaking in the same Atlantic article, attributes this optimism to the 1960s when NASA first put a man on the moon: "The optimistic and focused national goals of the Apollo program, coupled with the program's generous funding profile, set the foundation for an organizational culture that believes nothing is impossible despite significant technical hurdles and other challenges". And this mindset is still embedded inside the agency today.

"When asked to define 'project success,' nearly all the project managers we interviewed responded that a project was successful if it achieved its technical performance goals," the 2012 report said. "No manager mentioned controlling cost and schedule growth as significant measures of success. Moreover, all described their projects as successful even though many had experienced adverse cost and schedule outcomes."

# SUBTRACTION

Martin says NASA employees call this cognitive dissonance the "Hubble psychology." The Hubble Space Telescope was not an immediate success when it reached space in 1990. The telescope took much longer to develop than promised, exceeded its budget, and launched with a defect in its primary mirror that took several missions to repair and maintain. But today, Hubble is considered a national - perhaps even an international - treasure, and its chaotic beginnings have largely been forgotten.

"As long as you bring back—as in Hubble's case—pretty pictures, all your cost overages and schedule delays will be forgiven," Martin says. "Because what's important is the science at the end, not how you got there, how messy or over budget or over schedule you've been. That may be somewhat of an overstatement, but that's sort of the mentality: that all sins will be forgiven if you bring back the pretty pictures."

This is the outcome the Webb team is seemingly banking on. Webb is worth the wait, program officials have said over and over again, while the costs have mounted, goalposts shifted, and the finish line has moved further away. They hope the payoff will overshadow the pains of the process.

The arrival of SpaceX, the aerospace manufacturer and space transportation services company founded in 2002 by Elon Musk, on the intergalactic business scene has meant that the limits of such a dogmatic blue-sky approach have been made all the more clearer. The beloved space agency's excessive costs and delays are being brought into the cold light of day as Elon Musk's private company continues to cut costs for space travel at enormous rates.

This combination of believing that the end justifies the means in the most optimistic terms  and fears for astronauts safety, is only further hindering the agency's abilities to innovate.

***

Blue-sky thinking is one of the main features of Intuitive Intelligence. It is the ability to have creative ideas unbounded by conditioned thoughts or beliefs. If you recollect, Intuitive Intelligence is the faculty that corresponds with the Blue layer. More than in adults, it is the faculty most seen fully realized in children.

Where Nokia floundered due to its obsession with logical-thinking and by basing its next steps on its past success recipe, Steve Jobs' took Apple further than any phone company that came before. This man, who transformed Apple from a small startup operating from a shed into a multimillion-dollar empire, developed the phones of the future by remaining ever child-like in many ways, with its lights and shadows.

A similar child-like attitude can be seen in NASA's "Hubble psychology", an attitude that paved the way for humans to reach the Moon, indeed. But that attitude can also get hijacked by the shadow-side of the Blue layer.

No doubts, it is a rewarding state to be in. One from which everything is possible, and from where new and bold ideas keep flowing in. We like to refer to this state also as the *Kidfulness* state, one where we are beyond our conditioning and are fully harnessing the power of Intuitive Intelligence to ideate limitlessly.

However, by ignoring the limitations of the Material World, we also avoid crossing the threshold towards the gross layers of awareness. And those are the layers where the Boon becomes an innovation, where the impact manifests.

Children are immensely creative, but they can be just as fickle and stubborn. Ready to leave anything they are doing halfway to chase a new intuition. Other times they can be persistent with something no matter the constraints of the reality around them. Those are both invaluable qualities in the ideation phase of any innovation endeavour. However, if we do not move past them and start building the configuration, the Boon that we worked so hard to receive may go wasted, as we see in the case of NASA.

When we operate from the Blue layer, we are rewarded with thrilling insights and intuitions. We see what was invisible before. And it is such a rewarding feeling that it is easy to get addicted to it. When that happens, we become engulfed in the ideation process, hopping from one insight or intuition to another, without adding the layers of substance needed to manifest the intuition into a tangible configuration. We may end up having ideas for the sake of ideating, losing connection with the reality of the challenge that sparked our journey in the first place. Until an external occurrence forces us back to reality, often in an unpleasant if not painful way as NASA's story taught us. When that happens, tensions arise, and we are thrown back to the realm of survival.

If we feel that we are not making any measurable impact despite having many powerful ideas, or we struggle to stay with one thing and keep the ball rolling until the work is done, or we fail to close what we have open, we are likely stuck in the shadow side of the Blue layer. If we perceive that the world does not understand us or can not see the potential of our inventions, again, we may be spinning around the shadow side of the Blue layer.

To unstuck ourselves from the shadow side of the Blue layer, we must start by reconnecting with our purpose. We must ask ourselves the often-uncomfortable "why" question. "Why do I do the things I do?" "What is the impact that we want to achieve?" "What is the meaning of our journey?" Getting clarity about why we began the Innovator's Journey in the first place is how we rekindle the connection with reality, thus creating momentum so that the idea can start its manifestation journey.

Finding the deeper motives behind our actions, however, may not suffice if we do not follow through with actions. That is why we also need discipline. The discipline to stay authentic to our journey's purpose and, in the end, to our Self. Even when it looks less exciting than chasing a new insight or intuition. When we move from the Mystical to the Ordinary World, things may seem dull and mundane. As we saw earlier, the steps of the Arrival Act are made of practice, research, learning, prototypes, and sometimes failures. Boredom can be the greatest threat to success. That is why we need discipline. We need meaningful rituals, habits, structures and operating systems that help us stay true to our purpose, to the meaning of our journey.

Meaning and discipline therefore is a helpful combination to unstuck ourselves from the shadow side of the Blue layer. The former without the latter is anaemic and fragile. While the latter without the former shallow and mechanical. However, when meaning combines with discipline, magic happens.

# Innovators who are
# untethered souls

*Genius and madness have something in com-
mon: both live in a world that is different
from that which exists for everyone else.*
Arthur Schopenhauer.

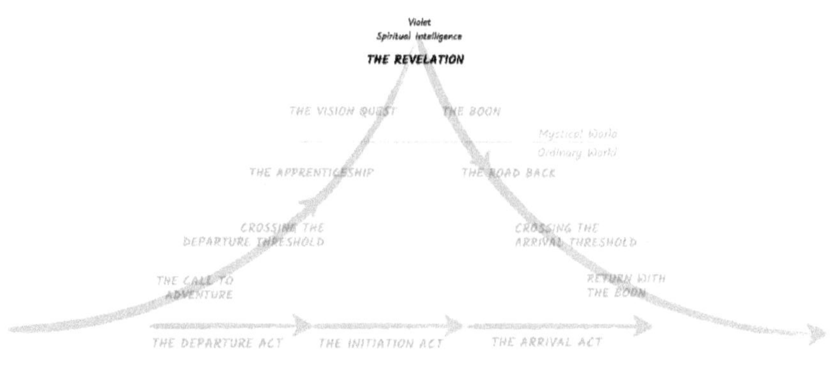


In the 19th century, there was a widespread belief that genius, in the sciences but especially in art, was strongly connected to insanity. This belief convinced Emile Zola to offer himself to science, so he could be studied and analysed while alive to explore the nature of this connection between genius and madness. For almost a year, French psychiatrist Édouard Toulouse and his team applied all their knowledge and tools, including methods usually used on asylum patients, to dissect Zola's mind.

They did not leave any stone unturned scrutinizing every aspect of Zola's physiology, appearance, thinking, life, and working habits, including details like his facial wrinkles and workspace.

At the end of his year-long study, Toulouse defined Zola as a neuropath with an unbalanced nervous system. Zola was delighted with the results of the investigation. At that time, everyone was expecting writers, and artists in general, to show some degrees of mental instability as a sign of a creative mind unbounded by the cold logic of reality. For Zola, Toulouse's conclusion was a form of recognition of his right to be included among the creative geniuses of his time.

The origin of this connection between genius and madness goes way back in time. It has its roots in ancient Greek. In his writings, Aristotle wondered why those who achieved remarkable results in philosophy, politics, poetry or the arts clearly showed signs of mental instability, some to the extent of mental illness.

History is full of tales that cast doubts on the mental sanity of many universally recognised geniuses.

The Greek mathematician Pythagoras was killed by his attackers because he refused to enter a bean field. His vegetarian philosophy prohibited him from eating or even touching beans. So when he found himself stuck between a group of assassins and a bean field, he decided to die rather than escape through the field.

Poor and recluse, Nikola Tesla, the great Serbian-American inventor accredited with a litany of innovations spanning a multitude of areas of science, died alone in New York City in 1943, shortly after declaring his love for a pigeon. "I loved that pigeon as a man loves a woman, and she loved me." Tesla would say of the white female dove. Such declarations would come as a surprise to his acquaintances because, despite his genius, Tesla was a staunch germaphobe.

Isaac Newton thought it was a good idea to use himself as a guinea pig for his experiments on optics, so he poked himself in the eye with a needle.

Edvard Munch, the famous Norwegian painter, suffered from depression, agoraphobia, and nervous breakdowns. At the upper left corner of his famous painting "The Scream" - that is said to have emerged from one of his hallucinations - he wrote in pencil the words, "Could only have been painted by a madman."

***

There are plenty of such stories for almost all greatest artists and scientists, hinting at a connection between high levels of genius and creativity, and madness.

In the last decades, researchers in different fields, from psychology to neuroscience, have explored this connection and found out that, indeed, such a link exists. An extensive study involving almost 1.2 million patients found out that mental illness is more common in artists and scientists compared to the population at large. Genius and madness are connected then, but they are not the same thing.

Albert Einstein, another universally recognized genius with a hint of apparent madness, once said: "I agree with Schopenhauer that one of the most powerful motives that attracts people to science and art is the longing to escape from everyday life."

Scientists, artists and innovators are motivated by the desire to escape from the status quo. Not only do they want a world different from the one that exists for everyone else, but they also imagine creating one different from that others believe in. Consequently, they are more open to embrace the Innovator's Journey through a consistent process of subtraction, removing their conditioning until they experience that moment of revelation. As we saw earlier, the peak of the journey is a blissful moment, one in which time and space dissolve, and we experience the wonder of being in a state of flow.

As beautiful and exhilarating as that moment is, artists, scientists and innovators intuitively know that they must continue their journey to realise the potential of that revelation. They must harness the other layers ' faculties and complete the manifestation process to make the imagined world a new reality.

Some, however, remain entangled, entirely or in part, in that feeling of total fulfilment at the peak of the Innovator's Journey. They end up lost in the shadow side of the Violet layer, a condition in which our inner experience is so detached from reality that it can lead to insanity, real or apparent. They might become one of those incredibly visionary people who keep talking about crazy ideas, who forget to eat or have no care for personal hygiene, or seem to not care about their relationships with others. They are people who live in a world that nobody else seems capable of understanding.

With many innovators, this is just a temporary phenomenon. One that, however, can have a lasting impact or define an entire career.

In his book about flow, Mihaly Csikszentmihalyi wrote that "the experience is so pleasurable, one wants to repeat whatever helped to make it happen." We know he is talking about flow, yet those words would fit in the description of any addiction.

In the 1950s, psychologists James Olds and Peter Milner conducted a test placing rats in a box where there was a lever that, once pressed, would deliver direct stimulation to a pleasure centre in the brain through implanted electrodes. The results were dramatic. Some rats would press the lever thousands of times per hour. The pleasure created was so high that it overshadowed all other natural stimuli. Rats forgot to eat and drink, females abandoned their newborns, some were willing to continuously cross an electrified floor just to reach the lever. Rats had to be physically re-moved from the box to prevent their death.

Similarly, the transcendence experience is so profoundly blissful that being in that state becomes the goal and not the way, to the extent where it can trigger behaviours related more to the sphere of addictions or mental insanity.

When that happens, the journey's peak becomes the destination, and a potential genius becomes that guy with crazy ideas.

When our paths cross with people lost in the shadow side of the Violet layer, we cannot interact with them in the same way we would with any-body else. There is great potential hiding in their expanded minds. They envision things that most of us cannot fathom. However, because they are disconnected from the Ordinary World, they can create tension. They may feel that the people around them cannot understand them, and to be hon-est, they cannot. At the same time, trying to keep them grounded can be stressful and disappointing.

To inspire innovators who are lost in the shadow of the Violet layer to embark on the return leg of the Innovator's Journey takes a careful ap-proach. Firstly, we must create a support system around such innovators where they can continue to remain a bottomless wellspring of visions, while others can distil these visions into ideas and manifest them into in-novations.

Secondly, and perhaps most importantly, we must connect them with the Ordinary World and help them establish a link to the potential benefi-ciaries of their revelations. That enables such innovators in finding a new balance reconnecting with the faculties of the grosser layers of awareness, releasing the potential of their genius minds.

## Integration Moment

If what we want is incremental or tactical innovation, we may get those results by bypassing parts of the Innovator's Journey and going straight into manifestation without getting to the Initiation Act.

However, often this bypassing is not the outcome of a deliberate action or conscious choice, but is due to our inability to access the faculties needed to move forward in our innovation journey. Due to our existing conditioning and blocks, our faculties may have been hijacked by the shadow-side of a particular layer, incapacitating us from accessing the other layers and their faculties.

Even unlocking all the layers and accessing the subtle and causal realms of the self is insufficient to deliver the boundless innovations we aspire for. It is only when we embrace the second half of the Innovator's Journey that we fully integrate the faculties of all five layers and realize the potential of our wholistic intelligence. Then we can source the *doing* from the *being,* and turn them into boundless innovations.

When we are trapped in the survival mindset of the shadow side of the Red layer, we react instead of responding to challenges with conscious choice. As we saw earlier, we become overly protective and territorial, sometimes at the expense of the people we serve.

The feel-good culture typical of individuals and ecosystems stuck in the shadow side of the Orange layer puts the emotional weight of the past over the present, hampering any momentum towards the future.

When it comes to innovation, Cognitive Intelligence played

a crucial role in humanity's achievements. However, this astonishing collection of successes can easily get us enthralled by the shiny shadow side of the Yellow layer. From there, driven by data, numbers and proof, we cannot go beyond what we can measure. We innovate only within the realm of probabilities, blind to the disrupting impact of what is unpredictable yet possible.

When we engage the Intuitive intelligence of the Blue layer we awaken the kidful power within us. However, if we remain trapped in the shadow side of the Blue layer and do not integrate our Intuitive Intelligence with all other intelligences, we may quickly slide into a childish attitude, one that finds thrill in constantly chasing one exciting idea after another than diligently manifesting one idea into something that has an impact. The shadow side of the Violet layer can turn the blissful feeling of the flow experience into an addiction. Experiencing the magic of that state can become the very goal of the journey, to the extent where we lose connection with reality. Being stuck in the shadow side of this layer can be perceived by others as abnormal, if not crazy.

## Self-enquiries:

- *Can you recognize yourself in any of the stories we shared?*
- *You can use the following table to assess if you are getting hijacked by the shadow side of any of the five layers. Do some of the following statements ring true for you or your ecosystem?*

| SHADOW SIDE | STATEMENTS |
| --- | --- |
| RED | Never change a winning solution or do not touch what is not broken<br>To materialize an innovation is the most important priority/responsibility.<br>Innovations that do not make an impact on our stakeholders are a failure<br>Getting the work done is what matters |
| ORANGE | The best decisions are the ones on which everyone agrees<br>Conflicts affect the quality of creative work<br>Nobody knows our work as well as we do<br>We are more creative when everyone is happy |
| YELLOW | A great decision is an informed one<br>To find the truth, we should stand clear of subjectivity<br>Knowledge is power<br>Emotions cloud our ability for strategic innovation |
| BLUE | Fail Fast, Fail Often<br>First-mover advantage is essential to success<br>Everything is a prototype (or beta forever)<br>Results do not matter as long as we keep pushing the boundaries |
| VIOLET | For innovation success, we must be ahead of time<br>We are way far ahead of the market and the industry<br>Numbers and data are secondary to innovation<br>Reality is just an excuse for lack of imagination |

# 3.4 Summing up the Innovator's Journey


Brian Froud

In Part II, we learned that by uniquely fusing all five intelligences into a higher form of *wholistic intelligence*, we can unleash the Being Innovator's potential. Thanks to the wisdom of the *Pancha Koshas*, we have learned that only through a process of subtracting the layers of our conditioning and expanding our awareness, can we access the subtle and causal realms of the self, thus opening a channel to the *causal library*.

However, unlocking the subtle layers is not enough to innovate. We must also integrate the faculties of all the five layers of awareness to fully manifest the potential of our wholistic intelligence. To do so, we must undertake the Innovator's Journey presented in Part III.

This comes with its own challenges. In the previous five chapters, we saw a few examples of what happens when we bypass part of the journey or we do not connect with all the layers of awareness. There are no doubts that there were people operating from all five layers in the organizations we wrote about; from creative geniuses who can source from the *causal library*, to brilliant scientists and super-efficient doers. However, because those different intelligences were not integrated or were fully skipped due to bypassing, they could not create the boundless innovations they had the potential for.

In summary, Part III brings together the five layers of awareness into an integrated innovation journey that every individual, organization or ecosystem MUST undertake in order to become Being Innovators and unleash the boundless innovation potential that lies hidden within them.

# Closing the Circle

*Innovation is an intentional human-driven change from something existing to something new that has an impact.*

The one above is the definition of innovation we introduced in part I of the book, a definition that identifies five essential attributes of any innovation. When a configuration is informed by all five layers of awareness, it can create boundless innovations that maximize all five attributes.

Innovation is *intentional.* It is the result of deliberate choices and actions. A humiliated Gandhi sitting on a bench, cold and alone at night in Pietermaritzburg, South Africa, decided that his job was to make a difference. So too, we must consciously choose to answer the call to adventure and begin the Innovator's Journey. Along the journey, that intention will transform from a destination to pursue into a destiny to live, making the resulting innovation radical.

Innovation is *human-driven.* Not only is innovation driven by human needs, but it also leverages human potential. Expanding our awareness is a subjective and deeply human process of liberation. Through that process, all five intelligences uniquely fuse into a higher form of wholistic intelligence. It also dissolves the distance between us and others, harnessing the power of our shared humanity to manifest boundless innovations.

Innovation *bears change.* It is inspired by what exists, rather than be limited by it. Change seems like a threat only when we operate from the grosser layers of awareness. However, when we integrate the subtle and causal layers of awareness, we recognize that change is natural. As the sages know, everything is constantly changing. We fully embrace impermanence and what may seem radical or disruptive to others becomes natural to us.

Innovation *catalyses novelty*: it must make the invisible visible, bring into reality something that did not exist before. However, sages are aware that the blueprints of all unrealized innovations are already available in the *causal library*. To access them we must unlock and integrate all layers of awareness. By reaching the peak of the Innovator's Journey and unleashing the potential of its wholistic intelligence, any configuration becomes a catalyst for novelty.

Innovation is *impactful*. Innovation is more than just making a change or creating something new. It is also about making a measurable impact. The magnitude of that impact is informed by what is at the center of our world. If we are the center, then self-preservation will drive our actions, and our innovation will be incremental at best. When we expand our awareness, our center widens until it will include everyone and everything. The resulting innovations, driven by a greater good, will be automatically radical and altruistic, leaving nobody behind.

# Epilogue

*The only hope for humankind is in the*
*transformation of the individual.*
Jiddu Krishnamurti

Boundless innovation is mystical in nature. It is an offspring of the union of human and the Divine. Einstein, Gandhi, Da Vinci, Tesla and other legendary innovators knew this.

Legendary innovators were mystical in their own unique ways. By now you must be convinced that mysticism is not an esoteric or religious concept. Mysticism is just the practice of accessing the subtler and causal dimensions of the self and expressing them. And that is where the secret sauce of boundless innovation lies.

When we expand our awareness and fuse all five intelligences into a higher form of wholistic intelligence, the distance between the Ordinary and Mystical Worlds dissolve, and we access a potential beyond what our limited human mind can fathom. We notice the Universe - God, the Super Conscious, Cosmos, Causal Self, Muse - conspiring with us to create something radical and altruistic.

This is the way of the Being Innovator.

Being Innovators are not cut from a different cloth. They are human, like anyone else. That means, every human can walk the Innovator's Journey and become a Being Innovator. We can do so by answering the call to adventure, turning our attention inward, and going through a very human journey of transformation.

Some choose this journey, while for some, the journey is thrust upon them. Whatever it is, beware. The journey is neither easy nor linear. It is a challenge-filled, unscripted and unpredictable journey that is highly personal, and can provoke strong inner duality and tension.

It is a journey for the daring, the adventurous, the courageous, the patient. You must slay your inner demons and soar like the phoenix from the ashes of your former self. And there awaiting you will be the same infinite fountain of innovations that have graced the lives of the great ones like Gandhi, Einstein or Da Vinci.

Most innovators bypass parts of the journey, thus limiting the full potential of the Being Innovator. However, the few who complete the whole journey would expand their awareness, discover more dimensions of the self, and transform their destination into destiny. At the end of the process, they are rewarded with boundless innovations.

As counterintuitive as it may sound, to complete the Innovator's Journey and expand our awareness, we need to embrace a process of subtraction; one that will allow us to remove all conditioning that holds us back from our immense creative potential. Only through this subtraction process will we be able to access the subtler layers of awareness, walk all the steps of the Innovator's Journey, and thus generate boundless innovations.

However, embarking on such a journey of subtraction is not an easy feat. Our society is rooted in the idea that we grow only by addition. We are told that we must invest a great deal of time and energy in gathering and accumulating theories, information, knowledge, techniques, skills and models, believing that within this massive database of accumulated knowledge, there would be all the answers we seek.

Innovations based only on these accumulated assets are bound by the past and limited by the condition of the human mind. They are, at best, a reshuffle of the past, if not mere continuations of the old.

Only through a process of subtraction can we reach that space of not knowing where, in J Krishnamurti's words, "there is this creativity which can express itself through various skills and crafts without causing further misery."

The process of subtraction requires us to turn our attention inward, beneath our configuration to reconnect with the self. By asking the questions for which we have no answers, something magical begins to happen. Our *doing*, sourced from the *being*, becomes boundless, making us almost superhuman. Our uniqueness shines through our configuration, infusing our craft with renewed energy. The resulting innovations, no more constrained by our conditioning, become boundless.

We become who we - and the world - have been waiting for; Being Innovators.

In ancient times, whenever a person set out on her grand journey of self-realization, the entire community gathered to bid farewell and celebrate the departure. Trusting that you are the next one in a line of *Mahatmas* (great souls) to embark on the Innovator's Journey, we gather around you with a prayer;

# SUBTRACTION

*The time that my journey takes is long and the way of it long.*

*I came out on the chariot of the first gleam of light, and pur-*
*sued my voyage through the wildernesses of worlds leaving*
*my track on many a star and planet.*

*It is the most distant course that comes nearest to thyself, and*
*that training is the most intricate which leads to the utter sim-*
*plicity of a tune.*

*The traveller has to knock at every alien door to come to his*
*own, and one has to wander through all the outer worlds to*
*reach the innermost shrine at the end.*

*My eyes strayed far and wide before I shut them and said*
*'Here art thou!'*

*The question and the cry 'Oh, where?' melt into tears of a*
*thousand streams and deluge the world with the flood of the*
*assurance 'I am!'*

-   Gitanjali 12, Rabindranath Tagore

# References

## Preface


P. 10: Wyndham, J. (1953). *The Kraken Wakes*. Penguin Books.


## Introduction


P.14: J Krishnamurti's quote is from *Krishnamurti in Paris 1950, Talk 3*

P.14: Jeong Kwang's quote is from Episode 1 of the 3rd season of Netflix documentary series *Chef's Table*


## 1.1 A World Shaped by Innovation


P.13: Floridi, L. (2014). *The Fourth Revolution: How the infosphere is reshaping human reality*(1st ed.). Oxford University Press.

P.23: "almost 1.1 billion fewer people are living in extreme poverty than in 1990 ", source: https://www.worldbank.org/en/publication/poverty-and-shared-prosperity

P.23: "life expectancy increasing by 20 years since 1960", source: https://data.worldbank.org/indicator/SP.DYN.LE00.IN

P.23: The World Economic Forum's quote from *The Future of Jobs, Employment, Skills and Workforce Strategy for the Fourth Industrial Revolution*, (2016). http://www3.weforum.org/docs/WEF_FOJ_Executive_Summary_Jobs.pdf

P.23: World Economic Forum. (2018). *The Future of Jobs Report.*http://www3.weforum.org/docs/WEF_Future_of_Jobs_2018.pdf

P.24: "Three billion of the planet's eight billion people use social media", source: *Number of global social network users 2017- 2025.* https://www.statista.com/statistics/278414/number-of-worldwide-social-network-users/

P.24: "an estimated 210 million people estimated to be suffering from either internet or social media addiction", source: Longstreet, P., & Brooks, S. (2017). *Life satisfaction: A key to managing internet & social media addiction. Technology in Society*, 50, 73–77. https://doi.org/10.1016/j.techsoc.2017.05.003

P.24: "college students who went to college after the year 2000 are considered 40%12 less empathetic", source: Konrath, S. H., O'Brien, E. H., & Hsing, C. (2011). *Changes in Dispositional Empathy in American College Students Over Time: A Meta-Analysis.* Personality and Social Psychology Review, 15(2), 180–198. https://doi.org/10.1177/1088868310377395

P.24: "close to 800,00013 people commit suicide every year ", source: World Health Organization. (2016). Suicide data. https://www.who.int/teams/mental-health-and-substance-use/suicide-data

P.25: "fifty per cent of the interviewed teens feel addicted to their mobile devices", source: *Technology Addiction: Concern, Controversy, and Finding Balance / Common Sense Media.* (2016). https://www.commonsensemedia.org/research/technology-addiction-concern-controversy-and-finding-balance

P.25: "The Syrian civil war, at the time of writing in its seventh year, was in part attributed to intense drought caused by the Earth's continued warming", source: Kelley, C. P., Mohtadi, S., Cane, M. A., Seager, R., & Kushnir, Y. (2015). *Climate change in the Fertile Crescent and implications of the recent Syrian drought.* Proceedings of the National Academy of Sciences, 112(11), 3241– 3246. https://doi.org/10.1073/pnas.1421533112

## 1.2 The Struggles of Innovation

P.29: The concept of innovation being an "auto-catalytic process" has been introduced by Jared Diamond in his book, *Guns, Germs, and Steel: The Fates of Human Societies*(20th Anniversary ed.). W. W. Norton & Company (2017).

P.30: "the share of people who identify themselves as spiritual", source: Wormald, B. (2015, May 12). *America's Changing Religious Landscape.*Pew Research Center's Religion & Public Life Project. https://www.pewforum.org/2015/05/12/americas-changing-religious-landscape/

P.30: "Almost paradoxically, this is particularly true for tech-savvy millennials", source: Newman, C. (2015, December 15). *Why millennials are leaving religion but embracing spirituality.*Phys.Org. https://phys.org/news/2015-12-millennials-religion-embracingspirituality.html

References

P.30: Data about the pharmaceutical industry from *Ten years on measuring the return from pharmaceutical innovation* report, Deloitte Center for Health Solutions (2019). https://www2.deloitte.com/content/dam/Deloitte/uk/Documents/life-sciences-health-care/deloitte-uk-ten-years-on-measuring-return-on-pharma-innovation-report-2019.pdf

P.31: Dyer, J. (2011). *The Innovator's DNA: Mastering the Five Skills of Disruptive Innovators* (1st ed.). Harvard Business Review Press.

P.32: "Nine out of ten startups, the heralds of innovation, fail", source: *Why Do Startups Fail? An Analysis of 3,200 High-growth Technology Startups.* (2013, October 30). Techli. https://techli.com/startup-genome-project/32391/

P.32: "only 6% of executives are satisfied with their innovation performance", source: *Innovation and commercialization, 2010: McKinsey Global Survey results.* (2010). McKinsey & Company. https://www.mckinsey.com/business-functions/strategy-and-corporate-finance/our-insights/innovation-and-commercialization-2010-mckinsey-global-survey-results

P.32: Data from the following Stanford Study: Bloom, N., Jones, C. I., Van Reenen, J., & Webb, M. (2020). *Are Ideas Getting Harder to Find?* American Economic Review, 110(4), 1104–1144. https://doi.org/10.1257/aer.20180338

P.33: More details on the survey of 270 corporate leaders on *The Most Commonly Cited Barriers to Innovation in Large Companies? Internal Politics.* (2018, July 30). Harvard Business Review. https://hbr.org/2018/07/the-biggest-obstacles-to-innovation-in-large-companies

P.33: "84% said that the organisation's culture was critical to the success of change management, and 64% saw it as more critical than strategy or operating model." Data from a Katzenbach Center Survey conducted on more than 22,000 executives in 2013

P.33: "70% of all change attempts fail to deliver the desired outcomes", source: Ewenstein, B., Smith, W., & Sologar, A. (2015). *Changing change management.* McKinsey & Company. https://www.mckinsey.com/featured-insights/leadership/changing-change-management

P.344: Dinopoulos, E., & Syropoulos, C. (2006). *Rent Protection as a Barrier to Innovation and Growth. Economic Theory,* 32(2), 309–332. https://doi.org/10.1007/s00199-006-0124-4

P.34: Data about the perceived decrease of the quality of life per country from: Poushter, J. (2017, December 5). *Worldwide, People Divided on Whether*

*Life Today Is Better Than in the Past.* Pew Research Center's Global Attitudes Project. https://www.pewresearch.org/global/2017/12/05/worldwide-people-divided-on-whether-life-today-is-better-than-in-the-past/

## 1.3 What is Innovation?

P.40: Anthony, S. D. (2017). *The Little Black Book of Innovation, With a New Preface: How It Works, How to Do It*(Reprint ed.). Harvard Business Review Press.

## Part II: Awareness Informs Configuration

P.45: Source of the opening story: McPherson, G. E. (2005). *From child to musician: skill development during the beginning stages of learning an instrument. Psychology of Music*, 33(1), 5–35. https://doi.org/10.1177/0305735605048012

P.46: Clear, J. (2018). *Atomic Habits: An Easy & Proven Way to Build Good Habits & Break Bad Ones*(Illustrated ed.). Avery.

P.46: the 'sucking sound of the core' has been defined by Scott D. Anthony in his book *The Little Black Book of Innovation, With a New Preface: How It Works, How to Do It*(Reprint ed.). Harvard Business Review Press. (2017b).

## 2.1 The Being Innovator

P.49: "a deficiency in any one of a number of factors dooms an endeavor to failure", source: Wikipedia. *Anna Karenina principle*. https://en.wikipedia.org/wiki/Anna_Karenina_principle

P.51: Sir Ken Robinson TED talk (2006, June 27): *Do schools kill creativity?*TED Talks. https://www.ted.com/talks/sir_ken_robinson_do_schools_kill_creativity

P.51: George Land TEDx Talks. (2011, February 16): *The Failure Of Success.*YouTube. https://www.youtube.com/watch?v=ZfKMq-rYtnc

P.51: "our capacity for perceiving information sits at around 11 million bits per second", source: Zimmermann M. (1986) *Neurophysiology of Sensory Systems.* In: Schmidt R.F. (eds) *Fundamentals of Sensory Physiology.* Springer Study Edition. Springer, Berlin, Heidelberg. https://doi.org/10.1007/978-3-642-82598-9_3

## 2.2 Configuration


P.54: Lewin, K., Heider, F., & Heider, G. M. (1936). *Principles of topological psychology*(1st ed). New York, London, McGraw-Hill Book Company, Inc.

P.57: "We can acquire knowledge through three distinct avenues: empirical observation, rational thought and introspection", source: Spira, R., Kastrup, B., & Md, Chopra D. (2017). *The Nature of Consciousness: Essays on the Unity of Mind and Matter*(1st ed.). Sahaja.

P.58: "75% of adults believe that they are not living up to their creative potential", source: *Study Reveals Global Creativity Gap.*(2012). Adobe. https://news.adobe.com/news/news-details/2012/Study-Reveals-Global-Creativity-Gap/default.aspx


## 2.3 Awareness Informs Configuration


P.61: Source for the opening story: ISTPP: Crime Prevention. (1993). Institute of Science, Technology and Public Policy. http://istpp.org/crime_prevention/index.html

P.61: New York Times article: *Meditating to Try to Lower Crime Rate. The New York Times.* (1993, August 1) https://www.nytimes.com/1993/08/01/nyregion/meditating-to-try-to-lower-crime-rate.html

P.62: "we are incredibly effective biophysical machines", source: Beauregard, M., Trent, N. L., & Schwartz, G. E. (2018). *Toward a postmaterialist psychology: Theory, research, and applications. New Ideas in Psychology*, 50, 21–33. https://doi.org/10.1016/j.newideapsych.2018.02.004

P.63: Kuhn, T. S. (2012). *The Structure of Scientific Revolutions*(50th Anniversary Edition) (4th ed.). University of Chicago Press.

P.65: Balasundaram, S., & Sathiyaseelan, A. (2016). A Comparison of Maslow's Theory of Hierarchy of Needs with the Pancha Kosha Theory of Upanishads. Artha - Journal of Social Sciences, 15(1), 59. https://doi.org/10.12724/ajss.36.4

P.66: *Plato and the Upanishads*, by N Kazanas, Omilos Meleton, Athens: January 2004.

P.71: Sull, D., & Eisenhardt, K. M. (2016). *Simple Rules: How to Thrive in a Complex World*(Reprint ed.). Mariner Books.

## 2.4 Anandamaya Kosha - The Violet Layer

P.78: Definition of flow from: Csikszentmihalyi, M. (2008). Flow: The Psychology of Optimal Experience(Harper Perennial Modern Classics) (1st ed.). Harper Perennial Modern Classics.

P.79: examples of "multiple discovery" or "simultaneous invention from: Ogburn, W. F., & Thomas, D. (1922). Are Inventions Inevitable? A Note on Social Evolution. Political Science Quarterly, 37(1), 83. https://doi.org/10.2307/2142320

P.81: Source of the research on social flow at St. Bonaventure: Walker, C. J. (2010). Experiencing flow: Is doing it together better than doing it alone? The Journal of Positive Psychology, 5(1), 3–11. https://doi.org/10.1080/17439760903271116

## 2.5 Vigyanamaya Kosha - The Blue Layer

P.85: Catmull, E., & Wallace, A. (2014a). *Creativity, Inc.: Overcoming the Unseen Forces That Stand in the Way of True Inspiration*(Illustrated ed.). Random House.

P.88: Abbasi, K. (2011). *A riot of divergent thinking. Journal of the Royal Society of Medicine*, 104(10), 391. https://doi.org/10.1258/jrsm.2011.11k038

P.88: Rochat, P. (2003). *Five levels of self-awareness as they unfold early in life. Consciousness and Cognition*, 12(4), 717–731. https://doi.org/10.1016/s1053-8100(03)00081-3

## 2.6 Manomaya Kosha - The Yellow Layer

P.99: Immanuel Kant, *Critique of Pure Reason*. Original title *Kritik der reinen Vernunft*, first published in 1781

P.99: Edward and May-Britt Moser research on the grid cells: Moser, E. I., & Moser, M.-B. (2008). *A metric for space. Hippocampus,*18(12), 1142–1156. https://doi.org/10.1002/hipo.20483

P.101: "natural language is a necessary condition for human beings to be capable of entertaining at least some kinds of thought", source: Carruthers, P. (2002). *The cognitive functions of language. Behavioral and Brain Sciences*, 25(6), 657–674. https://doi.org/10.1017/s0140525x02000122

P.102: Francesca Gino's article on HBR: *The Business Case for Curiosity.*(2020, November 6). Harvard Business Review. https://hbr.org/2018/09/the-business-case-for-curiosity

P.103: Tippett, K. (2017). *Becoming Wise: An Inquiry into the Mystery and Art of Living* (Reprint ed.). Penguin Books.

## 2.7 Pranamaya Kosha - The Orange Layer

P.107: "the power of technology benefited over 70 million rural83 households involved in milk production", source: Kurien, V. (2004). *India's Milk Revolution— Investing in Rural Producer Organizations.*

P.110: Sean Foleno's definition of Social Intelligence from: Ganaie, MY & Mudasir, Hafiz, *A Study of Social Intelligence & Academic Achievement of College Students of District Srinagar,* Journal of American Science 2015; 11(3)

P.111: The idea of making emotions work for us, instead of against us has been inspired by the article *What Is Emotional Intelligence, Exactly? Here's the Entire Concept, Summed Up in 1 Sentence* by Justin Bariso published in 2017 on Inc. website. Bariso's original sentence is: "Emotional intelligence is the ability to make emotions work for you, instead of against you."

P.113: Satell, G. (2017b). *Mapping Innovation: A Playbook for Navigating a Disruptive Age* (1st ed.). McGraw-Hill Education.

P.114: Collins, R. (1998). *The Sociology of Philosophies: A Global Theory of Intellectual Change* (Revised ed.). Belknap Press of Harvard University Press.

P.114: The concept of emotional contagion is taken from: Hatfield, E., Cacioppo, J. T., & Rapson, R. L. (1993). *Emotional Contagion. Current Directions in Psychological Science,* 2(3), 96–100. https://doi.org/10.1111/1467-8721.ep10770953

P.114: Definition of mirror neurons from: Kilner, J. M., & Lemon, R. N. (2013). *What We Know Currently about Mirror Neurons. Current Biology,* 23(23), R1057–R1062. https://doi.org/10.1016/j.cub.2013.10.051

P.115: Studies about the role of environments and places on people's ability to create and innovate: [1]Thoring, Katja & Gonçalves, Milene & Mueller, Roland & Badke-Schaub, Petra & Desmet, Pieter. (2017). *Inspiration Space: Towards a theory of creativity-supporting learning environments./10.21606dma.2017.19.* [2]Meusburger, Peter.(2009). *Milieus of Creativity: The Role of Places, Environments, and Spatial Contexts./10.1007/978-1-4020-9877-2_7. [3]Knight, G. K., & Marlow, O. (2016). Spaces for Innovation: The Design and Science of Inspiring Environments.* Frame Publishers.

[4]Clifton, Nick & Fuzi, Anita & Loudon, Gareth. (2014). *New in-house organizational spaces that support creativity and innovation: the co-working space.*

P.115: Definition of Vastu Shastra from: *Vastu Shastra [What Is It & How You Can Apply]*. Vastu Shastra Guru. https://www.vastushastraguru.com/

P.115: Definition of Feng Shui from *What Are the Basic Principles of Feng Shui?* The Spruce. https://www.thespruce.com/what-is-feng-shui-1275060

## 2.8 Annamaya Kosha - The Red Layer

P.117: Dyson's interview with Inc magazine, source: Mochari, I. (2021). *Try, Try Again: Lessons From James Dyson's Invention of the Vacuum.* Inc.Com. https://www.inc.com/ilan-mochari/vacuum- innovation.html

P.118: 2011 Dyson's article on Wired: *No Innovator's Dilemma Here: In Praise of Failure. Wired.*https://www.wired.com/2011/04/in-praise-of-failure/

P.118: Dyson, J. (2000). *Against the Odds: An Autobiography* (Business Icons) (2nd ed.). Texere.

P.119: Dyson's article in the Globe and Mail: *Yes, it's OK it took me 5,127 attempts to make a bagless vacuum. The Globe and Mail.* (2014) https://www.theglobeandmail.com/report-on-business/careers/leadership-lab/yes-its-ok-it-took-me-5127-attempts-to-make-a-bagless-vaccuum/article19992476/

P.123: Nitzsche's quote from: *Human, All Too Human: A Book for Free Spirits,* published in 1910 by T.N. Foulis. Originally published in German in 1878 as *Menschliches, Allzumenschliches: Ein Buch für freie Geister*

P.123: Duckworth A. (2018b). *Grit: The Power of Passion and Perseverance* (Illustrated ed.). Scribner.

## 2.9 The Wholistic Nature of the Being Innovator

P.129: Source of the Aldabra's story: esquireme.com. (2020). Esquire. https://www.esquireme.com/content/46133-an-extinct-bird-just-evolved-it-self-back-into-existence

# Part III: Awareness Fuels Innovation

## 3.1 Becoming the Being Innovator

P.1147: Campbell, Joseph. *The Hero with a Thousand Faces*. 1st edition, Bollingen Foundation, 1949.

P.147: Gennep, A., Vizedon, M. B., & Caffee, G. L. (1961). *The Rites of Passage*(First Thus ed.). University of Chicago Press.

P.149: Vogler, C., & Montez, M. (2007). *The Writer's Journey: Mythic Structure for Writers*, 3rd Edition (3rd ed.). Michael Wiese Productions.

P.149: Campbell, J., Cousineau, P., & Brown, S. L. (2014). *The Hero's Journey: Joseph Campbell on His Life and Work (The Collected Works of Joseph Campbell)*(Third ed.). New World Library.

P.152: Richard Feynman explains the feeling of confusion. (2007, November 3). [Video]. YouTube. https://www.youtube.com/watch?v=1ytxafTXg6c

P.155: "happiness is only real when shared" from *Into the Wild*, a 1996 non-fiction book written by Jon Krakauer on the life and death of Chris McCandless

## 3.2 How Awareness Fuels the Innovator's Journey

P.169: Lindley, P. (2017). *Little Wins: The Huge Power of Thinking Like a Toddler*.Portfolio Penguin.

P.169: Extract of Rainer Maria Rilke's letter from: Rilke, R. M., & Norton, H. M. D. (1993). *Letters to a Young Poet*(Revised ed.). W. W. Norton & Company.

P.174: Gray, D. (2016). *Liminal Thinking: Create the Change You Want by Changing the Way You Think*(1st ed.). Two Waves Books.

P.176: "Babies are born in blood and chaos; stars and galaxies come into being amid the release of massive primordial cataclysms", source: Pressfield, Steven, & Godin, S. (2015). *Do the Work: Overcome Resistance and Get Out of Your Own Way*. Black Irish Entertainment LLC.

## 3.3 The Pitfalls of Bypassing the Innovator's Journey

P.182: Fortune's quote from: Melanie Lindner (2010, May 6) *Proctor & Gamble lowered prices during recession. Fortune.*https://archive.fortune.com/2010/05/06/news/companies/Proctor_Gamble_cheaper_products.fortune/index.htm

P.186: Data about Kodak's decline from *Kiplinger's Personal Finance* magazine, Apr 1962. Read also https://www.forbes.com/1998/04/16/feat.html#2b8b8d9f3a44

P.193: Tricia Wang's article for Ethnography Matters: *Big Data Needs Thick Data. Ethnography Matters* Ethnography Matters (2013). http://ethnography-matters.net/blog/2013/05/13/big-data-needs-thick-data/

P.196: Hardy, B. (2019). *Willpower Doesn't Work: Discover the Hidden Keys to Success* (Reprint ed.). Hachette Books.

P.200: Statements by Lori Garver extracted from: Koren, M. (2018, August 31). *The James Webb Space Telescope and NASA's Culture of Optimism. The Atlantic.* https://www.theatlantic.com/science/archive/2018/08/nasa-culture-optimism-james-webb/566558/

P.208: "mental illness is more common in artists and scientists compared to the population at large", source: Kyaga, S., Landén, M., Boman, M., Hultman, C. M., Långström, N., & Lichtenstein, P. (2013). *Mental illness, suicide and creativity: 40-Year prospective total population study. Journal of Psychiatric Research*, 47(1), 83– 90. https://doi.org/10.1016/j.jpsychires.2012.09.010

P.208: "Genius and madness are connected then, but they are not the same thing", source: Simonton, D. K. (2005). *Are Genius and Madness Related? Contemporary Answers to an Ancient Question. Psychiatric Times.* https://www.psychiatrictimes.com/view/are-genius-and-madness-related- contemporary-answers-ancient-question

# Epilogue

P.221: J Krishnamurti's "there is this creativity which can express itself through various skills and crafts without causing further misery." from: *Krishnamurti in Bombay* (Mumbai) 1955, Talk 5

# About the Authors

Elliot Leavy is the former editor of the technology and innovation magazine MAIZE and editor of culture magazine BOZO. Through interviews and working with the likes of tech investors, CEOs, and Oxford academics, Elliot has a holistic understanding of the tech world today and tomorrow. He has also written for numerous publications across the globe focussing on politics, belief systems, and culture.

Fabio Salvadori is a coach who helps individuals, teams and organizations awaken their inner potential for innovation. He is a restless creative thinker who has spent twenty years in the tech industry, creating innovative services and products across different sectors, which earned him an Italian national award for innovation in 2007. His natural fascination for the elusive mechanics of human creativity pointed his exploration inward to find the spark that can make anyone an innovator. Fabio loves short poems, long conversations and dried mango.

Sujith Ravindran is a contemporary mystic and a serial author. He helps leaders, institutions and movements in the social, political and business domains access unforeseen realms of awareness and fulfil their true reason for existence. He is the founder of the *World Fellowship of Conscious Leaders* through which he today brings over 40 years of scholarship in spiritual sciences to contemporary fields, for which he was awarded the honour of Ambassador of Peace in 2012 by the Council of Assisi, Italy. Sujith sees life as a prototype and likes to fiddle with all aspects of his day-to-day living. He loves hot peppers.